E-Therapy

A. L. Kitselman

published in the USA and the UK
by

MASTERWORKS INTERNATIONAL
27 Old Gloucester Street
London
WC1N 3XX
UK

Email: admin@mwipublishing.com
Web: http:/www.mwipublishing.com

ISBN: 978-0-9565803-7-5
copyright © A. L. Kitselman 1953, 2013

Cover by mywizarddesign.com
© Morag Campbell/Chrisharve/Dreamstime

*This book is intended as a reference manual only, not as a medical
text. Anything suggested herein is not a substitute for needed
medical care.*

Contents

Publishers Preface   5

Introduction to the New Edition   8

Invitation   16

Approach   17

Asking   21

Turn-off   31

Fire   35

Tremolo   41

Posturing   43

History   44

Strategy   51

Argument   58

E-Plus   68

E-Minus   73

Qualifications   79

A. L. Kitselman (age 22)   88

Original Edition   After page 89

The words 'I am' are potent words;
be careful what you hitch them to.
The thing you're claiming has a way
of reaching back and claiming you!

A. L. Kitselman

Publishers Preface

MWI Publishing is pleased to reprint the first volume in what will build to become the Kitselman Collection comprising of all the writings and audio lectures of A. L. Kitselman.

In 1950, psychotherapist, physicist and mathematician A. L. Kitselman wrote a book called E-Therapy whilst working in Honolulu. Uniquely, the book was hand written and self-published. Whilst we have transcribed the original into a modern typeset form for ease of reading, we have included the original hand written form in the second section of the book, which we feel gives a more personal connection to the man and his work.

Kitselman was one of the pioneers of Cognitive Therapy, which was just beginning to change the face of modern psychiatry in the early 1950s. He had developed E-Therapy during the 1940s from his studies in psychology and of the great religious philosophers, whom he called the Time Teachers[1]: Kakusanda, Krishna, the Rishi Kapila, Lao Tsu, Gautama Buddha, Jesus Christ and Krishnamurti.

Although E-Therapy dates from the 1950s at the start of a burgeoning period of self exploration and self development, which came to be known as 'the human potential movement,' E-Therapy is as relevant today as it was then. Much of Kitselman's approach to what he calls 'integration' is still the basis of modern day therapy, and all of the physical effects of successful E-Therapy can be witnessed in some of today's energy based forms of bodywork. Kitselman was also one of

1. The Time Teachers by A.L. Kitselman was published in 1939; the culmination of six years of study.

the first people to publicly promote the work of Dr Carl Rogers, the acknowledged founder of 'client' or 'person centred' psychotherapy, also known as the 'humanistic approach.'

Kitselman's invitation on the first page of this book strikes a chord as we realise that today we are still searching for ways to increase personal happiness, achieve inner calm and put an end to feelings of insecurity and fear, while increasing creativity and becoming more integrated human beings who are capable of achieving greatness.

Modern commentators have acknowledged that E-Therapy is a form of meditative therapy similar to the Jungian process of active imagination. The meditator, or to use Kitselman's term, the transient, is helped by the questions of an observer to assist the meditator to stand aside from the preoccupations of the ego. This allows for the opening of a wider consciousness and a deepening of inner awareness which facilitates contact with the well of 'inner knowing' that resides in us all.

The English writer Aldous Huxley, best known for his novel Brave New World, wrote that; 'his friend Kitselman, had evolved, out of the texts of early Buddhism, a form of therapy which he called E-Therapy.' Though not sure how it worked, Huxley was intrigued enough to work with E Therapy and stated that in the cases he had seen it had led to a 'remarkable increase in insight and improvement in behaviour.'

E-Therapy was used to great benefit in the 1970s, with children who had developmental and cognitive disabilities, by the educator Miss Clare Gay of Bexhill-on-Sea in Southern England.

Although they emerged around the same time, mistaken associations have been made between E-Therapy and L. Ron Hubbard's Dianetics. The two men did work together, for a short time, before Hubbard developed Scientology. In a letter from Kitselman sent to his colleague Max Freedom Long in 1953, he wrote; 'Also, on behalf of Mr. Hubbard and myself, I must ask you not to speak of E-Therapy as a form of Dianetics. Both he and I—he first—have emphatically stated that E-Therapy is not Dianetics.'

Masterworks International Publishing
Ireland

Introduction to New Edition

Suzette Kitselman

My Dad was a pretty cool guy. Alva La Salle Kitselman was one of the pioneers of Cognitive Therapy, or the 'talking cure', at a time when mental illness was being treated with lobotomies and electroshock "therapy". Here's how that came about: He was born in 1914 in Battlecreek, Michigan, and raised in Muncie, Indiana. His father, A. L. Kitselman Senior, was the man who patented and manufactured the first steel roller skates, by putting the ball bearing into them, and also invented and patented machines that weave wire fencing out in the fields. This was towards the end of the westward expansion, when everyone was staking their claim on lands west of the Mississippi and needed to fence them in. Alva's mother was a journalist and writer in a time when proper ladies didn't do such things! So theirs was a house of forward thinking.

Papa's IQ had been tested before he was ten, and it was pretty high up there, but he never liked to discuss that. He was reading at a very early age, and by the time he was eight, his fingers could span the octave on the piano. He played classical piano concerts in the region, being billed as a child prodigy. But his interests were elsewhere.

Being the son of such a successful industrialist, "Beau" Kitselman had every comfort possible, yet he was unsatisfied by this. He didn't really enjoy being "Little Lord Fauntleroy" as he called it, one of the richest kids in town, because he saw the inequality of it all. Christianity didn't answer his questions about life. When he was nine, he would often go to the local mission (which unbeknownst to him, was partially supported by his own family), dressing shabbily so as not to be recognized, and eat his only meal of the day with the poor and the unfortunate. As a little boy, he was mesmerized when the owner of the only Chinese restaurant in town would go to the phone on the wall in the dining room and speak another language into it. When Papa realized there were other languages in the world, he realized there must be other ways of thinking as well. This began his lifelong journey of study into many languages, religions, belief systems, our need for belief systems, and our capability for psychological healing, wonderful growth, and achievement. He became a scientist at a young age, and also studied chemistry, physics and mathematics as well. Integrating science and the teachings of the Prophets of many religions, he later developed E-Therapy in the 1940s.

From Muncie, my dad went to study at Columbia University in New York, MIT in Boston, and Babson Institute near Boston. In New York, he founded The Institute of Integration; a forum for discussion and study, for the purpose of enlightening and aligning to our own higher selves. The members examined religions, philosophy, science, and world cultural and political matters. Then Papa went to Stanford University, in California, where among other classes, he attended a class in Sanskrit, the ancient language of India, the last year it was offered. There were only three people in that class. He also fiddled with radio broadcasting, chemistry, physics, higher mathematics, psychology, and other pursuits at Stanford. King Prajadhipok of Siam presented Stanford with a gift: a reprint of an Indian encyclopedia entirely in Sanskrit, which had been originally written about 4500 years ago. Stanford gave them to my dad, because he was the only one who could read them. Understanding that there is a lot of lost knowledge in the world, Papa began to read the encyclopedia, with articles on everything from the life of Buddha, Hindu gods, sex, metallurgy, to physics and other scientific theorem. Years later, on his lecture tours, he often told other scientists about these ancient physics discoveries, which he told me were parallel with 'new' physics discoveries and theory just emerging in the 1970s. Several of his peers encouraged him to publish this information in Scientific American, but the journal would not consider it, because my father did not have a PhD. Just before he passed away, he was beginning work on a translation of the volume on physics from this ancient encyclopedia.

During World War II, he worked with the Department of Defense, on various top secret operations; the Philadelphia experiment among others. Years after he passed away, our family was informed that he had done some covert operations as well, although he never told us about them. We know he monitored the German submarines off the coast of Virginia for a time, listening to their coded messages and interpreting for the military. Then he was sent to Hawaii to work at the military base at Pearl Harbor on various scientific studies and experiments. 1951 found him doing tests on human psychic capability for the military. There were five people in the room. Two were being tested: one person under the influence of LSD, and one person not under that influence (as a control). There was also an assistant, my father, and a "government observer". Essentially, the military wanted to determine whether LSD made one psychic, in which case they were going to send spies to the Soviet Union and they would use the drug for espionage and intelligence gathering! The "government observer" later instigated an investigation against my dad for "Un-American Activities" during the McCarthy era, which is funny, because he had no idea he was being investigated until the Freedom of Information Act was passed, and we requested all the records on him. When the package arrived, in 1971, it was a stack of paper eight inches tall, with most of the text on the pages blacked out. But he and I were able to read enough of those pages to see that the government wasn't sure what to make of A. L. Kitselman!

Does LSD make one psychic? Papa's answer was no, although it does make one much more sensitive. So they didn't send spies on LSD to Russia. Later, he did his own testing on subjects under the influence of peyote and other natural hallucinogens to determine if they helped with past life regression therapy.

While in Hawaii, he became familiar with the psychotherapy work of L. Ron Hubbard and eventually became the executive officer of the Dianetics Foundation in Honolulu for a short while. Before going to Hawaii he had discovered the work of Max Freedom Long and his 'Huna' movement. He introduced some of Max's huna terminology into E-Therapy and E-therapy was accepted wholeheartedly by Max's Huna Research Associates (HRA's). Because of this, many incorrectly link E-Therapy with Scientology or Dianetics. In newsletters from the Huna group, my father made it very clear that E-Therapy is not Dianetics, and that neither man, Hubbard nor my father, wanted to be linked to the other in any way. My father had been working on E-Therapy since the 1940s, well before they met.

In fact, a famous family story tells of Hubbard coming for dinner at our house. The two men sat in the living room and talked late into the evening after dinner. Mr. Hubbard told of his plans to develop Dianetics into Scientology, basically a series of long, very costly courses, with many 'levels', which take a long time to finish, with the goal of making a person 'clear.' Hubbard also said that he intended to define Scientology as a religion. Papa disagreed with Hubbard's plans on many different points of principle and promptly escorted him out of the house. That was the end of their friendship, although Hubbard tried to rekindle it more than once.

The Kitselman family had owned Pyramid Lake Ranch, at Pyramid Lake, Nevada near Reno, at the Paiute Indian reservation since 1936. From Hawaii, Papa moved back there in the early 1950s, where the Institute of Integration flourished with visitors and salons focusing on human capability, E-Therapy, and eastern philosophies and religions. Many years later, he said that at the request of the US government, he was also observing the skies for UFOs, after the Roswell incident, and in connection with Area 51.

From there we moved in 1958 to La Jolla, California, (before it had attitude) where the Institute of Integration continued, and we spent many happy years there at the seaside. During those years, he was asked by the US military to improve upon the new defensive weapon: the anti-ballistic missile (ABM). If a hostile country launched an Intercontinental Ballistic Missile (ICBM) to strike the US or its allies, this weapon chases the offending missile in the sky, locking onto it and following it until it catches up and destroys the threat in midair. The original software for this tracking mechanism gave the ABM the ability to follow its target by readjusting its trajectory every 8 seconds. When Papa rewrote the software, the missile would readjust its trajectory every 6/10ths of a second, making it much more agile and accurate in tracking, overtaking, and exploding its target in mid-air. Some of this software design was later developed into the synchronized flight we see now in the Blue Angels exhibitions, when multiple aircraft lock into flight with each other.

He taught his children that all the major religions basically teach the same thing: that we should all pursue our connection to our higher self, the master, the inner voice, the saviour, the aumakua, the bodhi, God, Buddha, Jesus, our soul, the all-knowing, the inner voice, our intuition, 'I've got a hunch,' 'something tells me,' our superconscious, or 'whatever you want to call it.' Since there are many names for this, and the name to be used depends on the person and their cultural orientation, he used "E" when referring to this, and the appropriate word is to be verbally filled in during E-Therapy sessions. He said that all the religions had their Prophets, those who spread this word, in various ways and times throughout history. He further told us that it was man who often corrupted the message, that we all have a direct connection to this, and that we don't need to go to an organized house of worship to get it. This last bit was a little too revolutionary to put into his books at the time. He also taught us not to deify anyone to the point of our own blindness.

He often had E-therapy sessions in our home, for free; and did lecture and book tours quite often as well. As a young girl, I realized he was becoming somewhat known when three college boys drove down to San Diego from Canada, without an appointment, just to meet him, during the social revolution of the 1960s. They arrived early one Saturday morning, and since Papa was up writing computer code until 6am most days, he was still asleep. When I told him about our guests, he got up to meet them, and they spent the entire day and evening talking in the living room together. The visitors stayed for dinner, slept on our living room floor, and left early the next morning.

Papa was one of the early writers of Fortran, an early high performance computer programming language and created lots of software back when only scientists had computers. The house and garage were full of IBM printouts and IBM computer cards with lines of numbers and little square holes punched in them. There were stacks and stacks of papers covered in handwritten numbers all over his computer room, and in drawers everywhere. He had a typewriter and used the hunt and peck method of typing. The University of California, San Diego, used his software in the supercomputer there, and in exchange he used the supercomputer. We would often go there together when I was very little. The supercomputer took up a room as big as a football field, it seemed to me, and had rows and rows of glassed-in refrigerated computers with tape heads spinning inside and lights blinking. He would set me up to play hangman on one of the earliest computers, while he 'computed' as he called it, and communicated with other scientists all over the world on the telex.

He was a very pleasant man, with a gentle sense of humor and respect for everyone. He loved powdered sugar on his Shredded Wheat. He was always writing, often in numbers. He took his family on long road trips to places like the Grand Canyon or a mountaintop observatory or Mexico. We always sang songs on the way. Once when we were driving somewhere, I asked him what he was thinking about. He said, "See that license number on that car over there? That number is the square root of….." Another time he answered the question this way, "Do you see the lines of sediment in these rocky mountains? I'm thinking about the time, millions of years ago, when the earth's crust was pushed together to form these mountains in the first place." He was always full of amazing observations and perspectives. He taught us to think outside the box before many of us knew there WAS a box that we had been thinking in. When he met someone new, he would try and guess at the origin of their last name, and learn something about the culture of that individual. He is remembered by many for his kindness and generosity. At the dinner table, he would ask the children, the youngest to the eldest, "What did you learn in school today?" From there, the conversations would blast off into subjects like reincarnation, religion, what God is, physics, and politics. Nothing was off-limits.

I would often come home to find him working in his home office, and ask him what he was working on. One particularly memorable answer was, "I'm working on a mathematical function that is half way between addition and multiplication." I'm told now, by a scientist working on this project, that the new Quantum computers being developed will utilize this new function, and other mathematical and physics work he did, to accomplish things only dreamt of in science fiction movies. What this computer will do is something most would not believe possible in our current world.

Welcome to your discovery of E-Therapy!
I hope you enjoy this book, and the other volumes to come.
Suzette Kitselman
June 2013

INVITATION

Would you like to improve your conduct? Is there a habit you'd like to get rid of?

Would you like to experience extreme physical pleasure? Intense, ever-fresh happiness? Deep impartial calmness?

Would you like to lose the feeling of insecurity? Make an end of doubt and perplexity? Lose all sense of fear, hatred, and grief?

Would you like to become a prodigy in science, government, business, art or education? A genius in originality, mental grasp, or in understanding others? Would you like to develop supernormal powers?

Would you like to become fully integrated? To be directly aware of things (without needing to sense them or think about them)? To realize a state of being in which there is no obstruction?

These pages tell how. They tell of E-Therapy, which is the simplest and most effective method of personal integration known to me at this time.

A. L. Kitselman

APPROACH

Greatness exists in every person who can recognise greatness. He who composes, and he who appreciates, a great symphony are equally great in appreciation; the difference is only that the composer can construct what both can appreciate. Greatness is passive in both, while active in only the composer. All persons who fully appreciate a great work of art are potentially as great as the maker thereof.

So also with the works of literature, science and philosophy. He who can admire a revolutionary mathematical proof is potentially as great as the originator thereof. All who can find delight in the works of Whitman, Newton or Emerson are potential Whitmans, Newtons or Emersons.

The problem is how to transform the potential into the actual. Greatness is in us; how can we let it out?

It is the purpose of these pages to show that greatness can let itself out; it need only to be asked. It is no exaggeration to say that both the method and its results are little short of miraculous.

What is this method?

It can take a thousand forms. One extremely simple approach is for one person to say to another, "Let us ask your mind to take whatever steps are necessary in order to remove whatever is obstructing it. Relax, close your eyes, and let's see what happens."

In some cases such a procedure will bring results never experienced before - such interesting results as have been mentioned.

Two conditions seem to be essential:

a. There must be a request for action, and

b. The transient (the person experiencing the process of transformation) must passively watch what happens.

This second condition seems to be helped in most cases by having another person present to make the request and to watch how things go, so that the transient will remain passive and attentive. This other person seems to act as an energizing observer, so to speak, and may be called the 'observer'.

The experiment conducted by transient and observer is called a 'session,' and may last a few minutes or a few hours. Sessions are usually about one hour long.

Now, that part of the mind which removes obstructions may be called by any name the transient prefers. It has been called the 'examiner', the 'integrator', the 'purifier', the 'decontaminator', the 'master', the 'observer', the 'fellow inside', the 'natural clearing mechanism', the 'great one', the 'wise man', the 'inner voice', the 'witness', the 'perfect one', the 'saviour', the 'messiah', the 'redeemer', the 'ideal', the 'Lord', the 'sage', 'Sri Krishna', 'the pure one', the 'protector', the 'teacher', the 'integral', the 'omniscient', the 'holy spirit', the 'comforter', the 'buddha', the 'over-soul', the 'higher self', the 'super-mind', the 'super-ego', the 'ultra-mind', the 'transformer', the 'all-knowing', the 'buddhi', the 'prajna', the 'bodhi', the 'aumakua', 'something tells me', 'I've got a hunch', and 'Rover'. Since the name to be used depends upon the transient, we shall write "E" whenever this part of the mind is meant, and the proper word is to be verbally filled in.

An E-Therapy session, then, consists of
a transient with a certain knowledge of E
an observer with a certain knowledge of E
and work done by E; five factors are involved.

What can E-Therapy accomplish, and how long does it take? The list of possible accomplishments has already been given (see invitation), and the length of time required to bring about a desired change depends upon the five factors just mentioned. If transient and observer are both in good health, and each has a good understanding of E, then spectacular results may be expected within a few hours.

The case of Mrs. C. P. is an illustration of this. In August 1950 she was depressed and irritable as a consequence of going back to college at age 35 while trying to cook, wash, and keep house for her husband and two young daughters. Her college work was extremely difficult for her as she had forgotten how to study. She was unable to take part in a required swimming course because of a deathly fear of water. Despite all her efforts she was failing in her studies, and she became so irritated with her children that she frequently found herself yelling at them.

At this point her husband repeated a one-paragraph invitation to E (which he had just heard over the telephone), and she went into a one hour E-session which was accompanied by a feeling of extreme physical and emotional well-being. Since this first session she has enjoyed such remarkable emotional richness that she frequently feels the skin-tingling thrills and flashes of ecstasy which most people experience only in their youth. In the eyes of her friends she lost five or ten years, both in appearance and manner. This one session ended her depression and reduced her irritability to such a point that she found herself yelling at the daughters not more than once a week. Nevertheless, she still had difficulty with her studies, as before. At intervals of five days she was given five more one-hour sessions, and her grades have moved from the B-C-D range to the A-B range. Whereas formerly she used to study slowly and laboriously, reading with poor comprehension, making many notes and painstakingly memorizing them, she now reads quickly and easily, makes no notes, and memorizes nothing. When examination time comes, she attends without special preparation, mentally calls upon E to help her, and finds that she can answer any question instantly if she has read the answer at any time. She had lost her fear of water and is the star of her swimming class. She got one degree with such ease that she is continuing her studies in order to get another. Six hours of E did this.

As to what this miracle-working E really is, it is important to learn this from experience rather than make theories about it. There seems to be an endless variety of such experiences, as well as an endless variety of theories about E. The ordinary mind seems to deal with specific things in a simple, step-by-step way, while E appears to handle whole groups of things simultaneously and in a manner that is both subtle and wondrous. The ordinary mind is full of opinions, motives, and compulsions and has limited fields of interest and action; E is not conditioned or compelled in any way and does not seem to be interested in limited fields or abilities. The ordinary mind and E co-operate in us, although they are different in character. The nature of this co-operation is something to think about, and what this particular kind of thinking does to us is also something to think about, for it is the gateway to all that is wonderful.

ASKING

Why is it that E will help a transient when asked to do so? Why is it necessary to ask? If E has the power to help, why doesn't he help without being asked? If E has always dwelt within us, why aren't we perfect already? If there is really a miraculous transforming intelligence within us, why weren't we all perfect years ago? If E has done nothing for us up till now, why start now? Isn't this whole business rather ridiculous?

Suppose that your next-door neighbor was a wise man. Unless you had wisdom yourself, you wouldn't know that your neighbor was wise. He would make no effort to tell you about his wisdom for conceit is not a part of wisdom. He would not be interested in showing you the error of your ways, for he would be free from the missionary impulse. Though he might have many wondrous powers, they would be invisible to you. You might easily live next door to such a man for ten, twenty, or thirty years without ever suspecting anything out of the ordinary.

Suppose something threatened you in some way. Your wise neighbor might easily protect you with his wisdom, but would you realise that he had done so? It isn't likely. Even in times of calamity you might be helped without knowing it, for wisdom does not advertise itself. How, then, would you ever find out that your neighbor was wise?

Only by asking. Ask a wise man to help you understand yourself, and he is at your service instantly, for self-knowledge is the beginning of wisdom. Ask him about anything else and he will ask you why you want to know, thus directing you back to the task of understanding yourself. Only on rare occasions will he discuss any other subject.

Of course, few of us have a wise man living next door, pleasant though that might be. All of happiness might come from such an association. Yet in each of us there is a wise man who lives much closer than next-door, as wise as the wisest man who ever lived, as wise as wisdom itself. We call this a wise man within us "E", and we say that E is that part of our own mind which is clear and wise. But who knows what E is? Perhaps only E knows; we can make many theories. It is important, however, that we have either no theory or several; to have one theory is to pretend to know. Theory or no theory, E does do a great many things, and it is useful to know what E can do.

Now we can answer the questions with which we started. E will help a transient when asked to do so because a transient is a seeker of self-understanding. It is necessary to ask because E has no desire to interfere with the transient's independence. E doesn't help without being asked, except in an emergency and secretly, because it is important for us to use such intelligence as we have. Though E has always dwelt in us, we are not thereby made perfect because it has not previously occurred to us that perfection is either possible or practicable. Although there really is a miraculous transforming power within us, we were not perfect years ago because we didn't know about E or what E can do. Though E may have done no recognisable wonders for us to-date, E will start now because we are asking it; we are asking for self-understanding now. And, finally, for these and other reasons it is decidedly not correct to say that this whole business is ridiculous. E-therapy is something that works.

How, then, does it work? How does one become a <u>transient</u>, or an <u>observer</u>?

Reading these pages will turn a <u>static</u> or inert personality into a <u>transient</u> or changing personality, for whoever reads these pages must give <u>some</u> thought to E, and E responds to the slightest touch.

There are many, however, who cannot read these words. How are they to be helped? How does one act as an <u>observer</u>?

To act as an observer, let the candidate for E-transformation read this material, or tell the substance of it in your own words. See that your candidate understands the general idea of a subconscious mind which is inferior to the conscious mind, and a super conscious mind which is superior to the conscious mind. An anecdote or a question about mistaken identifications (such as the poverty-bred idea that being rich equals happiness) will serve to illustrate the sub conscious mind, while a super-normal mental phenomenon (such as the unconscious solving of problems or the ability of a mental prodigy) will illustrate the superconscious.

This general introductory material should be presented simply and without argument. When you discuss the subconscious, <u>don't</u> talk about the theories of Mesmer, Braid, Freud, Jung, etc., And when you mention the superconscious, <u>don't</u> <u>talk</u> about the theories of Rhine, Hubbard, Kitselman, Werthauer, Altman, Fisher, etc. And don't talk about your own pet theories, either. Theories have no place in this preliminary discussion; let your measure of what is acceptable be Whitman's maxim, "Only what nobody denies, is so."

This means that you must avoid positive and unsupported statements, most of which cause instant controversy. Suppose you start out by announcing authoritatively, "Freud discovered the subconscious mind; Kitselman discovered the superconscious mind." An uninformed person will be entirely unimpressed, never having heard of either man or either mind. An average person will be intimidated by your statement and attitude; this will be a barrier between you. An informed person will classify you as a nincompoop because neither announcement is true except in a limited frame of reference, and because, even in that familiar area, many other heads were involved in each discovery.

Furthermore, don't claim that the three minds are a unit (or that they aren't); some people are greatly disturbed by such over-simplifications. And don't talk about the views of Theosophists, Rosicrucians, and Anthroposophist's, etc. If the views of these groups were helpful in achieving personal integration, we would all have become Theosophists, Rosicrucians, or Anthroposophists long ago. The simple fact is that personal integration does not depend on any thesis that there is (or there is not) life after death, or that things are (or are not) predetermined, or that virtue is (or is not) rewarded. Personal integration is to be experienced, not believed in; kindly leave beliefs out of discussion.

If you like, you can compare the subconscious, conscious, and superconscious to the spectrum of light—infra-red, visible, and ultra-violet—. This is a handy way of straddling the question of whether they are one, or three. The thing to remember is that your transient must understand something about what goes on in E-therapy. Your job in this preliminary discussion is to provide this understanding without raising any points of controversy.

Here is a practical example of <u>asking</u>:

Have you ever had the experience of suddenly understanding something about yourself that you had never understood before?

Oh, yes—many times, I suppose.

Did you ever discover that one of your personal actions or attitudes actually had its origin in some silly misconception?

Yes, I did. For years I had a guilty feeling each time I went past an electric powerhouse. One day I realised that I had been gruffly ordered off the premises of a power station when I was just a little boy. Now power stations don't bother me at all.

That's an excellent example of the sort of thing we are concerned with in E-therapy.

You mean that your whole purposes is just to get rid of misconceptions?

Yes. All we want to do is get rid of the many mistaken identifications which exist in your mind. As we see it, each identification removed will make you feel just that much better.

Well, it's certainly true that I felt guilty near powerhouses because I still identified powerhouses with an angry, accusing voice. And it's also true that the guilty feelings disappeared as soon as I saw the light—that is, as soon as I saw how silly the identification was and thus removed it. But aren't we normally unconscious of our identifications? How do you propose to get at mine?

The same way you did.

The same way I did? What do you mean? All I did was suddenly realise that something was silly—or is that all I did?

What else do you <u>think</u> you did? Why did you have a sudden realisation on that particular day?

I don't know. I suppose I began wondering why power stations upset me, and then, all of a sudden, I <u>knew</u> why.

Had you ever before wondered why power stations disturbed you?

Now that I come to think of it, I never had—I had just accepted that they did.

What made you think of the childhood incident which originally caused your misconception?

Ah, that's the real mystery! I had completely forgotten the incident—hadn't thought of it in years, in fact. I've often wondered why I happened to remember that particular incident at that particular time—just when I needed it.

Yes, that's the mystery which led to the discovery of E-therapy. There seems to be some part of the mind which has the power to remove identifications. It was this part of your mind which caused you to wonder why power stations disturbed you, and then obligingly furnished the answer.

That seems remarkable, if there really is such a power in the mind.

Well, you'll soon be able to find out for yourself about that, because "E-Therapy" is just a name for the work that power does. We think that there is an intelligent power within you which can transform you by removing identifications, and we call this power "E", or whatever name you prefer.

Certainly, if there is any such power in man, it should be called "the Redeemer" or "the Saviour" or some such great name. However, "E" is good enough for me.

All right, then, "E" it is. "E" is our name for the intelligent transforming power within you, and "E-Therapy" is the work E does. Would you like to start now, and let E go to work?

I'm willing. What am I supposed to do?

Lie down, close your eyes, and just watch to see what E will do.

———————————

Now, some conversations such as the foregoing is all that is necessary to start an E-session. The observer will find information on the various activities of E in the sections which follow, and to which these remarks are an index:

If the transient reports a lessening of some tension or activity in the mind, refer to the section entitled TURN-OFF.

If an especially pleasant feeling or experience is reported, refer to the section on FIRE.

If a more-or-less violent agitation of the body or sense-impressions is experienced, refer to TREMOLO.

If changing postures, body motions or facial grimacing is observed, refer to the POSTURING section.

If incidents are remembered or recalled either fragmentarily or in complete detail, refer to HISTORY.

If the situation is presented in which the transient is apparently expected to do something, refer to the section on STRATEGY.

If the transient says "Why doesn't E start working?" or voices any other criticism or objection, refer to the section entitled ARGUMENT.

If E communicates only rarely and is unable to do much, study the E-PLUS section.

If E seems unable to operate in any way, study the section on E-MINUS.

It may be well to point out here that each and every action of E which is discussed in these pages has been observed in transients who did not know what to expect. E is the one who originated E-Therapy; Kitselman, Nowell, Patnoude, Murphy, Werthauer, Schuman, Altman, and Pinsker are simply the eight first observers of what E can do, the word "first" here meaning only "in the limited frame of reference attendant upon the apparent discovery by Kitselman (observer) and Nowell (transient) on August 28, 1950 in Honolulu". We have learned since that E has been discovered many times before, an excellent example of observer-less E-therapy being found in the book "I Say Sunrise" by Talbot Mundy, who <u>died</u> several years <u>before</u> Kitselman and Nowell made their 'discovery'. Other clear examples have formulated some aspect of E-Therapy—one as far back as 1250 B.C. Nevertheless, it is doubtful that the present widespread interest (scores of thousands of persons) has been seen before within historical times.

E-Therapy, then, is not the product of suggestion; everything E does will appear in some transient sooner or later, whether suggested or not. Yet it may appear <u>sooner</u> if the transient knows about it. For this reason it is in order to explain the powers of E to the transient. The example we have given of <u>asking</u> might then conclude as follows:

.... *Would you like to start now, and let E go to work?*

Won't you tell me, first, just what sort of things I can expect to happen?

Certainly. We have observed ten powers in E. They appear in people whether we tell them about them or not, but it is sometimes helpful to know something about them.

<u>First</u> is the <u>power to recognise causes</u>. What motives never lead to a pleasant consequence? What motives never lead to a painful consequence? What are the consequences of thinking something is permanent? What are the consequences of thinking some one thing, person or idea is happiness? What are the effects of identifying with something, of having definite ideas about the 'self'? What are the consequences of removing fixed identifications about permanence, happiness and the 'self'? What is the effect of fixed opinion? E is equipped with a full understanding of these matters, and can make it clear to you

Second is *the power to judge actions*. What is the effect of dissipation? What follows the struggle to get rich? What is the consequence of seeking power over others? What is the result of striving for a reputation? What are the after-effects of killing, stealing, sexual misconduct, dishonesty, slandering others, and so on? E has an understanding of actions and their effects, and can communicate it to you.

Third is *the power to measure behaviour patterns*. What is the effect of banking as a mode of life? If a man is a preacher, what will it do to him? What is the effect of conventional domesticity? What are the consequences of becoming a Trappist, a politician, a juggler, a communist, or a dress-designer? E knows all this, and can tell you.

Fourth is *the power to understand structure*. What is the person? What factors compose it? What is the exact structure of the body? What are feelings? What is memory? What are motives? What is consciousness? What is matter? What is life? What is its origin? What is its goal? It may seem hard to believe, but E seems to know the answers to all these questions, and can use them to straighten out any structural difficulty.

Fifth is *the power of insight into character*. How many kinds of people are there? How do they differ? What kind of person is this? Can he or she be trusted? Will this person get along with that person? In addition to knowing these things, E knows all facets of your character and can bring them into proper harmony.

Sixth is *the power to measure tendencies*. Which are the forces which change a person? How can this tendency be weakened, and that one strengthened? Is this person's character improving or degenerating? How can a man or woman be induced to change for the better? E knows all this, and will proceed to regulate your tendencies for best results.

Seventh is *the power to produce attainments*. What extraordinary experiences are possible for a person? What are the various levels of understanding? What are the degrees of emotional integration? How can pure ecstatic pleasure be experienced? What is ecstatic happiness, *and how can it be reached? Is there such a thing as ecstatic calmness? Can one achieve permanent freedom from perplexity, fear, conceit, and grief? E knows all about these attainments and can cause you to experience them.*

Eighth is the power to investigate history. What were you doing on August 28, 1950? What was your birth like? What happened during the first year of your life? Did your father and mother fight before you were born? Did you ever live before? All this E knows and can show you in various ways

Ninth is the power of extra-sensory perception. It has been found repeatedly that one E can communicate with another—and this to so perfect a degree that it is difficult to decide whether there are many Es or just one. Your E can communicate with my E, apparently, and this may help us in our work. E can also show you many things which have never been apparent to your senses.

Tenth is the power of infallibility. How well you can communicate with your E seems to depend on you, but, subject only to that one limitation, everything E does is right. No E has been known to make a mistake. E has no fear, no conceit, no ignorance, and no carelessness that we can detect.

If you're willing to ask E to help you, just lie down, close your eyes, relax, and watch these ten powers in action!

TURN-OFF

If some tension or activity of the mind seems to be suspended for the time being, this is what is called turn-off. After asking has been completed, the observer should wait three or four minutes. Then, if nothing has been announced by the transient, the observer may ask:

What seems to be happening?

If the transient's answer is like one of these:

Nothing seems to be happening.
I can't think of a thing.
My mind is a complete blank.
The worrying I've been doing has suddenly stopped.
There doesn't seem to be anything going on.
My, this is restful!
I've never seen my mind so quiet.
How peaceful it is!

Then E is using turn-off, and the observer may make some remarks such as the following:

You appear to be experiencing what we called turn-off. It is as if E has <u>turned off</u> *the normal flow of mental impressions. Most E-sessions begin with this turn-off, which normally lasts five or ten minutes or more. Turn-off is often our first evidence of the power of E, because very few people can achieve this condition without the help of E. The fact that you are experiencing it indicates that your E* <u>can</u> *communicate, and that your case is well under way, for many persons have received great benefit from turn-off alone.*

As to why E makes use of this turn-off, it may be that E likes to start with a clean slate, so to speak, and thus wipes the mind clean of all preoccupations before going further. Or it may be that the energy ordinarily consumed in the flow of mental impressions is now being saved up, in order to show you something later on. Or it may be that this is what you are like when the most active and intelligent part of your mind is busy elsewhere—that is, outside your range of consciousness. Any one or all of these explanations may be the true state of affairs; we do not know.

In any event, turn-off is comfortable and good for you. Enjoy it as long as E permits, even if it lasts through the entire session. Do not be impatient for something else to happen; turn-off alone is miracle enough. And don't worry about me; during long waits my E frequently puts me in to turn-off along with my transient. Just take it easy. At exactly the right time E will end the turn-off and proceed to something else. Until then, relax and enjoy what you are now experiencing.

Although turn-off is apparently one single state of being, E has the power to turn off (and on again) many different conditions of the mind. Turn-off maybe momentary (as during part of the session), temporary (lasting an entire session or for a few days or weeks), or permanent (this involves E-minus attainments). In E-sessions the following processes have been turned off:

Pleasure-craving (for tobacco, alcohol, sex, etc.)
Annoyance (anger, hatred, antagonism, etc.)
Mental inertia (slowness of mind, mental sluggishness, etc.)
Distraction (excitement, worry, fear, panic, etc.)
Perplexity (doubt, indecision, uncertainty, etc.)
Ignorance (obtuseness, stupidity, confusion, etc.)
Boredom (apathy, ennui, etc.)
Pain (physical, bodily pain is meant here)

Thinking (inquiring and willing)

Ecstasy (physiological; see the FIRE section)

Happiness (mental, emotional, aesthetic, etc.)

Perception of appearances, resistances, diversity, awareness of space

Awareness of awareness

Awareness of 'nothing'

Awareness of 'not being aware'

(Some of these may sound strange, but they do occur, and you may encounter them.)

Permanence-identifications (this is permanent)

Happiness-identifications (this is happiness)

Self-identification (this is the self, it is mine, etc.)

Delighting in something

Wanting something

Pursuing something

Taking up some pursuit

Material-identifications (this is substantial, material, solid)

Ambition-identifications (strain and strive for this)

Security-identifications (this is safe, constant, reliable)

Object-interest (this object is interesting, curious etc.)

Motivation (this is the real purpose, motive, aim, etc.)

Object-acceptance (this object is real, important, essential.)

Truth-acceptance (this is the final, certain truth)

Delusion-acceptance (false ideas of reality)

Protection-acceptance (here I am safe from danger)

Over-simplification (thoroughness is not necessary here)

Bondage-acceptance (I want to suffer and be limited)

Ideological fixations and effects (conditions, motives and tensions which results from adopting a fixed theory of reality)

Now what are ideological fixations? Are they such widespread and current ideologies as fascism, communism, socialism, capitalism, etc?

Yes, of course—but these are only secondary ideologies. The basic ideological fixations are oversimplified views of reality which are arrived at by disregarding whole areas of observation—speculative beliefs such as occultism, materialism, determinism, agnosticism, mentalism, theism, atheism, sectarianism, survivalism and racism. E seems to take the position that any one of these extreme opinions will cause inflexibility of mind and obstruct the process of integration.

If you are more interested in your beliefs than you are in becoming integrated, it will be best for you to stop at this point, for uncritically accepted beliefs are a bar to personal integration. It will not be possible for you to become a fully integrated communist, fascist, capitalist, or sectarian; fully integrated persons cannot be described with such labels. The best thing to do is to recognise your beliefs as speculations and postpone definitely accepting or rejecting them until you are fully integrated, for surely you will be able to decide more effectively then.

FIRE

If the transient reports:

I feel a pleasant tingling accompanied by ecstatic thrills and flashes. It moves through me in waves and there are jolts of pure ecstatic energy in it. I'm full of it; I feel it in every cell.

Or any portion thereof, or

I see something very beautiful or hear, feel, perceive, sense, know etc., or

I feel something very strongly. (neutral or pleasant) then the observer may conclude that E is using what is known as fire, and may say:

Your E has the power to bring you certain intensifications of feeling which are very beneficial. These experiences are sometimes startlingly vivid, but never are harmful. Relax and enjoy what you are experiencing, for it will do you much good.

The word 'fire' is used in this connection because it has been used for a long time to indicate strong feelings or emotional intensity. Thus we speak of 'playing with fire', 'the fire of passion', being 'fired with enthusiasm', being a 'spitfire' or a 'firebrand'; there are similar idioms used in ancient Sanskrit, Chinese and Pali.

Ecstatic fire involves physiological ecstasy which may appear in one or several or all of five forms:

Skin tingling (with 'goose bumps', body hair on end, etc.)
Thrills or flashes
Waves
Jolts or tremors (feelings of 'levitating force', etc.)
Saturation ('a non-sexual orgasm in every cell')

Tranquil fire is not accompanied by physical ecstasy; it features a quiet sense of happiness. The pleasant feeling in tranquil fire is mental, rather than physical.

Neutral fire contains neither ecstasy nor happiness; it is an intensified feeling of poised neutrality between pleasure and pain, happiness and unhappiness.

Ecstatic fire is apparently the antidote for pain; within certain limits, a transient experiencing ecstatic fire cannot at the same time experience physical pain, a pinch being felt only as pressure and so on. When ecstatic fire is accompanied by turn-off of inquiring and willing, it is impossible to experience unhappiness. E has been observed to relieve and remove pain and unhappiness by 'turning on' ecstatic fire, and the urge to dissipate is reduced in those who have access to ecstasy, for it is itself the most intense of all physical pleasures.

Pleasure and pleasure-craving are transcended by tranquil fire, for it is the experience of intense happiness without need of pleasure. E has been observed to relieve and remove excess pleasure-craving by 'turning on' tranquil fire.

Transients who progress so far as to experience much tranquil fire may become too preoccupied with their new-found happiness, and neutral fire is a remedy for this, for it is the experience of intense awareness without need for happiness.

It is interesting to observe how thoroughly E provides for the emotional integration of the transient. It has been said that we are mentally and emotionally controlled by four drives —those toward

Physical fulfilment	(personal),
Emotional fulfilment	(relational),
Mental fulfilment	(associational), and
Ultimate fulfilment	(transcendental).

Now the emotional realization of these goals is to be found in four principal kinds of fire which E seems inclined to produce in every transient who enjoys good neuro-endocrine health. The mental attainment of these four goals will be discussed in the E-minus section; here we are concerned with the four kinds of fire.

What are the four fires?

The first is ecstatic fire associated with thinking (inquiring and willing), and it contains the four factors <u>thinking</u>, <u>ecstasy</u>, <u>happiness</u> and <u>intensity</u>.

The second is ecstatic fire with thinking turned off, and it contains the three factors <u>ecstasy</u>, <u>happiness</u> and <u>intensity</u>.

The third is tranquil fire, and it contains the two factors <u>happiness</u> and <u>intensity</u>.

The fourth is neutral fire, and it contains the two factors <u>neutrality</u> and <u>intensity</u>.

How do these four fires fulfill the four drives?

The first fire makes plain, everyday living seem a great adventure, for it involves turn-off of pleasure-craving, annoyance, mental inertia, distraction, perplexity, ignorance, boredom and pain.

The second fire is the heart of ecstasy, all thinking and unhappiness being turned off.

The third fire is the heart of happiness, for it does not contain the comparative grossness of pleasure.

The fourth fire is the heart of poised balance, for it is free from even the comparative grossness of being happy. It has another important quality, for it is said that the state of well-integrated emotional balance is the basis of true objectivity and permits knowing and seeing things as they really are.

Thus the first drive (toward physical fulfilment) is satisfied by the first fire, which is a condition of ecstatic living and thinking.

The second drive (toward emotional fulfilment) is satisfied by the second fire, which is a condition of pure ecstatic pleasure.

The third drive (toward mental fulfilment) is satisfied by the third fire, which is pure happiness.

The fourth drive (toward ultimate fulfilment) is satisfied by the fourth fire, which is pure awareness.

It must be understood that fire is not always at full intensity; sometimes it is quite weak. Fire and turn-off always appear together; there is no fire without turn-off, and there is no turn-off without at least some fire. This is because turning off any one activity of the mind causes an intensification of the remaining activities, and intensification is a synonym for fire. Thus when a condition opposed to fire is turned off, a complementary condition favourable to fire is turned on. In the preceding section we discussed some of the activities which E can turnoff; in this section we are discussing some of the activities which E can turn on. If transient doesn't like the word 'fire', replace it with 'intensity' or 'turn-on'.

In order to correct certain conditions of emotional inhibition, E has been observed to turn on four fire-purified attitudes toward living beings.

The first pure attitude is simple affection, which is equivalent to what is meant by the word 'love' when thought of as distinct from pleasure-desire and possessiveness.

The second pure attitude is compassion, which is genuine concern for those in trouble.

The third pure attitude is sympathy, which is rejoicing in the accomplishments of others.

The fourth pure attitude is neutrality, which is regard for the independence of others.

These four attitudes involve some degree of fire—the first three being forms of the first fire, and the fourth being an aspect of the fourth fire. In a given transient, E may turn them on as directed toward one, several, or many persons— even toward humanity in general. This may also apply to one, several, or many animals—or even toward an entire species, depending on the nature of the case. E uses the four attitudes in helping many, but they are especially powerful instruments in the task of helping repressed and unsympathetic persons.

In some sessions E has shown the transient beautiful colors, such as a beautiful blue color, etc. Some transients have seen beautiful scenes and pictures, heard beautiful sounds or music, tasted wonderful flavors, smelled pleasant odors or perfumes, felt pleasant touch sensations, or thought beautiful thoughts. Such experiences, of course, are all forms of the first fire.

In E-sessions the following processes have been turned on:

Dispassion	(physical contentment)
The pure attitudes	
'Lighting up' of the mind	(brilliance, clarity)
Calmness	(imperturbability)
Examination	(study, scrutiny, evaluation)
Understanding	(penetration, insight, knowing)
Delight	(interestedness, enthusiasm, joy)

the four fires

Awareness of space
Awareness of awareness
Awareness of 'nothing'
Awareness of 'not being aware'
Suspension of feeling and awareness (total turn-off)
(The four awarenesses mentioned above are four abstract fire states related to the fourth fire.)

Insight into impermanence (changeableness, flux)
Insight into unhappiness   (being controlled by identifications)
Insight into non-identity   (dis-claiming, dis-identifying)
Insight into weariness   (of being subject to limitations)
Insight into dispassion   (the basis of fire)
Insight into ending   (identifications, unhappiness, pain)
Insight into releasing   (getting free from controls)
Insight into crumbling   (of all supposed solid realities)
Insight into futility   (of all specific purposes)
Insight into insecurity   (nothing is safe, constant, or reliable)
Insight into no-object   (objects are of secondary importance)
Insight into motivelessness   (it is spontaneity and creativeness)
Insight into emptiness   (no preoccupation is worth-while)
Insight into transcending   (no doctrine is final truth)
Knowledge and vision
of things as they are   (freedom from delusions)
Insight into danger   (no place or position is safe)
Insight into caution   (one must be thorough)
Insight into removing   (how to get rid of controls)
four attainments of permanent freedom from ideological fixations and their various consequences (see E-MINUS)

Fortunate indeed is the transient who experiences many of these forms of fire, for they constitute all that an individual needs in order to become fully integrated.

TREMOLO

Closely related to the phenomenon of fire is that type of reaction which is called 'tremolo'. This may appear as a violent trembling or shivering visible to the observer, or the transient may say:

I have a trembly feeling in my stomach.
My eyelids seem to be twitching.
I see flickering flashes of light.
There is a trembling in such-and-such a joint.
I just feel shaky.
Every so often I feel a sudden jolt.

Sudden jolts or jerks may be quite pronounced and may affect the entire body. It is important to note that tremolo proper is not accompanied by any feeling of pain, cold, or fear; when these are present, consult the section on HISTORY. If the transient is experiencing tremolo, the observer may say:

This is what we call tremolo, one of E's most useful tools. It appears to be literally a shaking free from controls and identifications, and sometimes it is very strong. It is our experience that tremolo is highly beneficial, so relax as much as you can and let your E set you free from everything that can be dislodged in this way.

Certain non-dissipative religious orders actually receive their names because of the frequent appearances of tremolo among them. Thus the disciples of George Fox, an English mystic and religious revolutionary, became known as "Quakers", and the name stuck because since they were pacifists, it also suggested 'quaking' with fear. The disciples of American leader Mary Ann Lee became known as "Shakers". Tremolo is therefore a natural equipment of those who are close to the attainment of fire, whether this condition is arrived at as a result of E's work or as a consequence of rigid avoidance of dissipation. Many persons experience tremolo during sexual intercourse, which, at its best, is a near approach to fire.

If the tremolo seems excessively strong, the observer may say:

Your E has the power to protect you from any excesses.

This is usually sufficient to reduce any superabundance of tremolo, but in very rare cases (sometimes when E's verbal communication is not well-established), the tremolo may reach amazing extremes, so that the transient may say:

I feel as if the energy in the universe were flowing through my hands!, (or feet, body, etc.)

The observer may quiet such extreme activity by taking hold of the feet or hands of the transient.

POSTURING

Just as tremolo is an agitation treatment, posturing appears to be manipulation of the body by E for therapeutic purposes. There are many forms of posturing. Screwing up the eyes or shutting them very tightly or frowning—these are common forms of posturing. So are deep or rapid breathing, moving a particular limb, and changing one's position. Not infrequently the transient will seem to indulge in a vigorous self-massage, although the results of this practice are so beneficial that we suspect the real masseur of being far more skilled than any transient.

Posturing proper is not accompanied by any sensation or emotion or mental impression when these are present, consult the section on HISTORY.

In some instances, posturing can be extremely vigorous, so much so that the first E-session in which posturing (accompanied by tremolo) was observed caused both observers present (Kitselman and Patnoude) to break out in a cold sweat, although the transient was not in the least alarmed. Posturing can also be amusing to transient as well as observer, as in the case where a grown man, who had been repressed in childhood, was impelled by his E to turn several somersaults on the bed used in the session.

HISTORY

What you are is the result of what you did with what you were—isn't it about time you stopped? What you will be is the result of what you do with what you are—isn't it about time you started?

Such maxims of causal thinking are characteristic of the view that we are the product of the past. Sometimes, however, faulty conclusions are drawn from this point of view, such as "Our troubles exist; they are the product of the past; therefore the past exists." This causes a mistaken identification to appear in the mind, for the word 'exists' refers to present time. It is more correct to say

There is no past.

There is no future.

There is only <u>now</u>.

Nevertheless, we do appear to contain in us a more-or-less complete recording of all that we have experienced in the past. Such recordings are available to us for reference purposes, but they are ordinarily mis-used because we identify ourselves with them in some way. For example, there is in you a recording of what you experienced last year. If you understood things correctly, you would realise that the person you were last year <u>does not exist</u>, is dead and gone. Not understanding this, you are apt to cling to last year's recording as being part of what you <u>are</u>; you <u>identify</u> with it. In this way you give the recording power over you, you tie yourself to last year, and thus lose your ability to live and act in present time. When circumstances resembling those you recorded last year confront you in present time, you will not face them intelligently—you will do what it is recorded that you did last year. Thus, as a result of identifying, you operate as a mechanical recording instead of as a living, intelligent person. Some people act almost entirely from recordings; almost all of us do so at times.

E has the power to play these recordings for us and to help us to dis-identify. The transient may seem to re-experience a past incident, and frequently this wonder is sufficient to show the transient that the incident is not real, it is only a recording, and therefore has no intelligent bearing on present time. In this way we are set free from our actions and reactions of yesterday. Some theorists maintain that this is the only way in which we are set free from yesterday—that is, by experiencing the recording of an incident and dis-identifying in detail. E, however, seems to feel that this is only one of several methods.

E seldom plays the recording of an incident at the normal time-rate; this seems to be too slow. An incident may be presented in terms of its important factors only; this procedure is very rapid. An entire series of related incidents may be indicated in this way in just a few moments; sometimes the transient is conscious of a chain of incidents all at one time. If a transient communicates well with his E, the observer may be pretty quiet when E is handling history, for E's communication with the transient is then at a mental speed and cannot slow down to a verbal speed. In fact, Es that communicate well seldom work as slowly as verbal speed.

Certain ancient authorities say that the conscious mind is simply a consequence of the subconscious mind and the superconscious mind; it is only a by-product of the two minds of which we are not conscious. The subconscious mind seems to be a mass of identifications; several thousand years ago it was known as the 'identifier'. The superconscious mind (or E) does not seem to contain any identifications; it is said to have the power to know exactly. If this is so, the task of the conscious mind is to attempt to reconcile identifications (which are never exact) with exact knowledge (which contains no identifications), certainly a futile undertaking.

It is important for the observer to understand how these three minds are spoken to. This can be learned from Max Freedom Long: The Secret Science Behind Miracles. Briefly, the subconscious mind, being inferior, can be told what to do; hypnosis and most advertising methods are methods of controlling the subconscious mind. The conscious mind is rational; it can be reasoned with. Discussion and conversation are means of approaching the conscious mind. The superconscious mind or E, being superior, is never told what to do or reasoned with; it is asked to help, prayed to, invoked.

Thus the observer who attempts to direct or control E-Therapy is not in touch with E at all; only the subconscious mind responds to commands. If E is treated as an equal and approached by means of reasoning and discussion, no E is reached; only the conscious mind responds to such treatment. The observer must realise that E is very wise and knows best what to do; otherwise he is not communicating with E. The subconscious mind obeys; the conscious mind reasons; E knows.

The most rapid and successful E-Therapy is presided over by observers who have decided long ago that E is far smarter than they are and that the observer's job is only to assist when necessary.

Many of us were taught in school that 'things equal to the same thing are equal to each other'. In the imaginary and unreal land of pure mathematics, this is a useful rule of thought, but unfortunately our schools did not teach us that, except in the world of abstract symbols, the above quotation is a principal cause of insanity. How is this so?

In the actual, real, moving world, no to things are equal, are they? No two real things can be identical or equal. (KAPILA) as the ancient Greek Heraklides said, "You cannot step into the same river twice". (KAPILA) It may also be said that you can't speak to the same person twice. Just now, for example, the <u>second</u> time you read the word KAPILA you were a person who had just read the word KAPILA; the <u>first</u> time you read the word you were not such a person. Such differences are not necessarily trivial. If the two words 'KAPILA' had been bullets, for example, this discussion might be much shorter.

This is no artful quibble; it is a serious statement of fact to say that your personality is a flowing, changing complex of interrelated factors. You are not the same person you were a year ago. You are not the same person you were yesterday. You're not the person who started reading this. Not only that, but the person you now <u>are</u> is the only one of you that <u>exists</u>; the person who started reading this is <u>gone, ended, non-existent.</u>

Until you understand this fully you will continue to <u>identify</u> with persons you once were but now are not, and this will prevent you from living intelligently in present time. The persons you formerly were <u>do not exist</u>, and although you have recordings of them for reference purposes, do not make the mistake of thinking that <u>you</u> are the recordings, for that is what we call insanity!

Persons who live almost entirely out of recordings are seldom aware of present time reality, cannot look after themselves, and so we lock them up. Most of us live out of recordings in moments of stress and conflict; that is why we repeat ourselves so much in family quarrels, playing the same recordings over and over again for years and sometimes even decades. A very fortunate few have reached the goal E seems to intend for us; they live fully and creatively in present time and never repeat recordings.

It may seem ridiculous that a rule learned in the study of mathematics could cause so much trouble in everyday living, in which so little mathematics enters. Mathematics, after all, is only a game played with symbols; why should a rule made for symbols have any influence over living realities?

Words are symbols too, you know. The two words 'KAPILA' previously quoted are equal, identical—just as $8 = 8$. Also, aqua = pani = water just as $8 = 4 + 4 = 2+2+2+2$. Two words can be equal in letters and/or in meaning. But no two real things are equal, so the world of words is an imaginary place like the world of numbers.

Numbers are sometimes applied to real things, but this is very dangerous. Do seven horses equal seven horses, for example? Only once in a great while, and the man who thinks otherwise should not deal in horses.

Alas! words are regularly applied to real things and few realise the dangers. Does Mary Smith resemble Mary Jones? Silly question, isn't it? Yet there are people who try to replace one Mary with another!

Nor is this verbal nonsense limited to personal problems. Why, for example, did Joseph Dzhugashvili become such a power in Russia? Partly because he adopted the name

STALIN which is the Russian word for 'steel'. One of his aides uses the name MOLOTOV which means 'hammer'. Poor benighted Russians you say. But could Theodore Underdunker become President of the United States? Or Cecil Reginald?

Your E is concerned with the words you <u>identify</u> with. The most tricky and dangerous ones are

I me my mine myself   you your yours yourself
he or she   him or her his or hers himself or herself

and your personal names.

We use these words as if they were immortal and unchanging, and they serve to <u>identify</u> us with our recordings. In all <u>your</u> recordings the central character is referred to as 'I' or 'me' by himself (or herself), as 'you' and 'he' or 'she', 'him' or 'her', by others. Thus these old recording <u>seem</u> to refer to you today, and it isn't easy for you to see that they don't. Furthermore, your recordings contain statements by other persons in which these same pronouns are used, and you may therefore have <u>identified</u> these statements as applying to you.

The transient's E plays recordings in order to show the transient that they are recordings, and to remove identifications. He has no other interest in recordings, and no interest in the past. E may play only snatches a recordings and the transient will appear to re-experience only bits of incidents, or E may remove identifications in other ways, without ever playing recordings. It is E who will decide to follow this course or that course, not the observer or the transient, and no session must be expected to resemble what has gone before. Observers who have been influenced by those who insist upon detailed playing of recordings as a SINE QUA NON of progress in integration must remember that E-therapy is conducted by <u>E</u> and on the assumption that E <u>knows</u> what to do. It is our observation that E is interested in recordings only in certain cases, and that ten minutes of FIRE may accomplish more than many hours of HISTORY.

If a recorded incident is only partially sensed by the transient, the Observer may say:

Your E has the power to enable you to sense this incident in full detail, if he wishes to do so.

or

Your E will show you this incident fully, if it is a wise thing to do at this time.

The observer must at all times remember that E is the expert in charge. Questions may be asked, if E permits. Most of the material presented in these pages was learned from watching Es at work, and asking them questions. Just as a young interne might assist a great surgeon at the operating table, so must the observer assist the transient's E. Both interne and Observer are eager to learn, anxious to keep out of the way, and ready to help in any indicated way. Either might ask an occasional question, but neither would ever dream of telling the great expert what to do.

As an observer gains experience, he will develop faith and confidence in the incredible efficiency of E and in the efficacy of E-Therapy. This confidence will keep him from talking too much, and he will realise that no E-observer with reasonable good sense will be more effective than any other E-observer with a reasonable good sense, for it is the transient's E who does the therapy. This is literally true in all typical E-cases, in which E communicates well with the transient, and sixty to eighty percent of all persons are typical E-cases. There is no occasion for snobbery among the E-observers.

STRATEGY

When it is impractical or inconvenient to remove an identification directly, E has recourse to strategy. In general, E-strategy is as follows:

The transient finds himself in a situation which E has constructed—that is, the transient has the experience of being somewhere, and this 'somewhere' is not a recording; it is a scene produced by E.

In this situation, E indicates that the transient is to perform some act—such as open a door, cross a bridge, climb a tree, throw a ball, etc.

For some reason, the transient finds this difficult to do, and says so.

Being coaxed and urged on by the observer, the transient succeeds in doing what E has requested.

These four elements—a situation, an indicated action, reluctance, and final accomplishment—constitute typical E-strategy. Although the situation which E produces is 'imaginary', it is not consciously 'imagined' by the transient, nor does he find it too easy to do what E indicates. Let us examine the notes of the first E-strategy case:

Date: September 3, 1950
Observer: A. L. Kitselman, who has observed five transients for a total of six hours of E-Therapy.
Transient: Preston A. Patnoude, who has been 'audited' for thirty hours of 'dianetic processing', a procedure designed by L. R. Hubbard to evoke the eighth power of E and control it

at will. Although Hubbard's method is often successful, it has failed completely with this transient. Patnoude, however, was the first observer of fire in E-Therapy (see page 19) on August 29, and witnessed the first appearance of tremolo and posturing on September 1 (transient: Mrs Nora King— observer: A.L Kitselman).

I just saw a door slam shut, very hard. It is sprung and wedged in place—it slammed so hard .... This seems to be the control circuits which keep me from recalling incidents............... As I was saying that, the door was barricaded with strips of wood nailed across it.

Look around. Perhaps you can find a hammer—a claw hammer, maybe.

There is a sledgehammer over here to one side.

Use it to batter through the door.

No, that doesn't work; I'm on the wrong side of the door. I only wedged the door in tighter.

Look around for a crowbar or something.

Yes, here's a crowbar—a nice heavy one.

See if you can pry the door open.

All right.............. (several minutes elapse) ....

How are things now?

I can see through the bottom corner now.

Can you get through the opening?

No, it's too small.

Well, do what you can to get the whole door open.

All right...... (several more minutes)........ The door just fell through and disappeared.

What you see through the door?

Just blackness—I can't see anything.

Go stand in the door and look through. What do you see now?

Nothing—just blackness.

See if there is a light switch.

Yes, I found one over here on the side.

Well, turn it on.

I did, but it didn't work.

Very well. Walk straight ahead now, and watch for a light.

All right............................. I've moved forward one step, and I don't see anything yet.

Take another step.

I have.

Don't hesitate; go right ahead. If, as you say, the closed door represented the control circuits which obstructed your ability to recall incidents, I think they are all cleared away now, and you can recall events without difficulty.

...... I just tested what you said, and you are right; I <u>can</u> recall incidents now. I'm walking ahead now.

What do you see?

I see a clip-board lying there ahead of me with a bunch of papers on it.

Go forward and pick it up—see what's on the papers.

They are notes of some kind—probably the things that have happened to me.

Look closely—what do they say?

It's all faded away now—my E seems to be through for the day.

How do you feel?

Fine.

(elapsed time; 30 minutes)

This first strategy case is more or less typical. The door which the transient saw was the first thing he had ever seen clearly in lastingly with his eyes closed. His struggle to pry open the door was very real to him, for although no external motion was visible to the observer, the transient's replies to questions were spoken as if he were perspiring and short of breath. Also, what E accomplished was also very real, but the transient could recall incidents after the session.

E frequently represents the whole catalogue of recorded incidents as a kind of 'hall of time', as in this case. This 'hall of time' may appear as a long tunnel or pipe or scenic railway or road; the observer's task is usually to coax the transient to enter and travel as far as possible.

Or, E's strategy may consist entirely of an 'obstacle course' of one situation after another, some of them quite childish. One transient, who had been dominated by an older sister when a child, was directed to 'murder' her in various ways in a number of strategy situations. Again, E may simply show a pleasant scene at the end of the session to indicate that all is well.

Strategy is simply a name for any and all special tactics employed by E, and it may take many forms. It is strategy, for example, to put the observer into turn-off so that he will not become restless and interfere with the transient's turn-off, as E frequently does. Special information is sometimes given to the observer by E, as will be shown in the E-plus section.

The observer must remember that E will decide whether or not the transient is to understand any special symbolism in the strategy situation. When in doubt, ask E what to do. If E presents a strategy situation but does not communicate well enough to say what is to be done, the observer must suggest whatever seems most likely.

Strategy is most successful when the transient uses all available strength of will and force of imagination in doing as E directs. E seems to use the will-power the transient produces in order to affect the forceful removal of deep-seated identifications which the transient cannot conveniently or comfortably face directly. Thus the indirect method of E's strategy is a very valuable and powerful aid in the work of personal integration.

ARGUMENT

It is not necessary for a transient to <u>believe</u> in E-Therapy in order to experience results; in fact, very few persons have any appreciation of the reality of E until they have experienced results themselves or observed them in a number of cases. Nevertheless, strong beliefs can block the work of E, and it is necessary to take steps to put such beliefs to one side during sessions. Any belief or opinion which questions the operation of E-therapy may interfere with the work of E. Suppose that a session begins with ten minutes of normal consciousness and then the transient says:

I wish my E would start to work, or
Why doesn't something happen? or
I sure hope I have an E.

These statements are the equivalent of saying

My E isn't working. It doesn't work. or
Unless something happens, I'm out of luck. or
I'd like to have an E, but I haven't got one.

The observer must counter such remarks with:
Are you <u>sure</u> your E isn't working now? or
Something <u>may</u> be happening <u>now</u>. or
Isn't that like hoping you have a brain?
It is not the observer's task to refute or defeat the objections of the transient; all that is needed is to induce the transient to suspend the objections until after the session. If the transient says:

This whole idea of a super-smart mind in me that I've never known about is perfectly ridiculous!

A tactful observer will reply

Yes, it does seem rather preposterous, I know. But we'll never really know whether or not it is ridiculous unless we test it with an open mind, will we?

This sort of thing is called 'argument' because in the transient's mind there is an argument with E-therapy which the observer must suspend until the transient's E can present his case; it is not an argument between transient and observer. All E asks is a trial; after the trial the transient may be the judge and render an opinion. It is simply not good practice to render a decision before a trial or without a trial.

A certain amount of argument takes place in the transient's mind long before any sessions take place; the questions on page 21 are typical. The transient's views are to be modified by the observer only in so far as they impede the work of E; otherwise they are not be challenged.

The original writing on E-Therapy was mimeographed in September of 1950 in Honolulu. It was based upon some sixty E-sessions in which some twenty-odd transients were observed by Kitselman and Patnoude. At this time E-Therapy was outlined as follows:

STARTING WORK
ASKING
TURN-OFF
EASY WORK
FIRE
TREMOLO
POSTURING
HISTORY
DIFFICULT WORK
STRATEGY
ARGUMENT

As these words were written E-Therapy was in its second year, and no alteration in the above structural outline had become necessary as yet. Familiarity with these three stages and eight factors is familiarity with E-Therapy.

In this outline, strategy and argument are labelled difficult work because they call for active participation on the part of the observer, participation in which skill and understanding are important factors. This skill and understanding may be acquired through patient observing of E at work and through the study of E-minus material. The following examples of argument and how to cope with it may be of assistance:

(Note: Use no more of the argument-countering material than is needed; the full treatment here given is required only in extreme cases. The observer's job is only to counter, not to instruct; E will instruct.)

Shouldn't I keep reporting everything to you?

Why should you? Might that not get in E's way? Why should I know any more than enough to tell me how things are going? Am I giving you this therapy, or is E? Shouldn't you be primarily concerned with your E, rather than with me? If you occupy yourself with talking to me, are you relaxing and letting E work? After all, your E is in charge here: if he wants you to report to me, do so; if not, just watch what he does.

I don't like this business of referring to E as a separate, independent mind.

Have we said, 'separate'? Where did you get the idea that your E is separate from you? Don't you see that if you think of your E as a separate entity, and then deny the existence of such an entity, your mind will reject automatically anything that E tries to do for you? If you seize upon reasons to reject E, are you giving him a fair trial?

We <u>do</u> say that E is more-or-less independent, but this is our observation, rather than a fixed theory. Many transients have found that they can experience turn-off or fire, for example, when they ask E for it, but not when they try to achieve these experiences without asking E. A few are able to experience turn-off or fire at will. Thus E appears to live independently in the majority of cases.

As you become better acquainted with your E, you can test these matters yourself and draw your own conclusions. In the meantime, suppose we suspend judgement until we can find out what <u>your</u> E can do for <u>you</u>. Let's throw all objections overboard and let E go to work.

In that section on <u>asking</u> you attempt to explain away a lot of objections to E-therapy by comparing E with a wise man. This visualizing of E as a wise man seems ridiculous to me.

Then don't visualise E as a wise man. The point is that there is a part of your mind which is free from motivations and which doesn't become active unless you furnish a motivation by consciously or unconsciously asking for help. This is not the easiest thing in the world to understand, and the personal illustration of a wise man living next door serves to convey this information. Everything in the section you mention can be understood in a de-personalized way if you prefer it. After all, a wise man may be assumed to be someone with a strong and active E, and the behaviour of a wise man as a person must resemble the behaviour of E as a part of the mind.

We do not know the nature of E. If there is something in us which opposes the work of E, this opposition is apt to take the form of convictions that E is personal or impersonal, organic or inorganic, physical or mental, etc., and rejection of E-Therapy on the basis of these convictions. Let's put such quibbling aside.

I object to this personifying of E as the examiner, monitor, integrator, etc., and the use of personal pronouns when referring to E.

Then refer to E as the examining, monitoring, integrating, etc., process or activity or function, and the use of the pronoun 'it'. Or, if you wish to avoid both extremes, use the term 'E' as both noun and pronoun.

E is an __aspect__ of a human being, a person, a man or a woman or a child. It has been indicated by several advanced E-transients that "E is what we are when there is turn-off" and that "turn-off is suspension of the identifying process". If this is so, it may be proper to refer to E in the same way that we refer to a human being, a person, a man or a woman or a child.

Again, E is observed to be an intelligence of extremely high order. If you think that such a high intelligence must necessarily be mechanical, inorganic, or abstract, then refer to E as 'it'. If you think that such a high intelligence must necessarily be human, personal, or organic, refer to E as 'him' or 'her'.

You are at liberty to refer to E in the way that suits you best.

I want to achieve such-and-such (supernormal recall, clairvoyance, healing power, artistic talent, increased earning capacity, release from some trouble, position, reputation, skill, etc.)

Doesn't this amount to telling E what to do? If you tell E what to do, you aren't talking to your E—although you may indeed be talking to some part of your mind which will get you what you want. There are many forms of faith healing and so-called 'mental science' which will sometimes get you what you want. Which is more important, to get what you want, or to achieve permanent personal integration? Asserting or affirming or imagining something may help you get what you want; but will not help you become integrated. Getting what you want without becoming integrated is far worse than becoming integrated without getting what you want. Becoming integrated, however, will solve all your problems, either by getting what you want or by getting rid of the want.

Let us concern ourselves, then, with asking E for help—without specifying. If what we want is wise, E will give it; if not, E will cure us of wanting it. First let us become integrated, and all other things will be taken care of.

I have decided that E is such-and such. (the astral body, the matrix of intentions, the atman, the unconscious, the guardian angel, a deva, etc.)

Perhaps you are right. However, it will be better for you to temporarily suppress this conviction of yours, because we have found that a fixed conception of what E is (even though it may be true) is likely to hinder E from working freely.

You see, your conception of E is a product of your mind, and, until you become fully integrated, a part of your mind consists of false information. Your conception of E maybe partially based upon false information, no matter how clear it may seem to you now. Such a conception is perfectly acceptable as a temporary opinion of what E is, but it will obstruct your personal integration if you see it as a certainty.

After all, it is more important for you to let your E give you therapy than it is for you to make theories about E. In general, it seems that transients progress more rapidly when they do not theorize about the nature of E. Theories usually are used in place of realities. Your E is here <u>now</u>; you need no theory about it.

It seems to me that the claims made on behalf of E-Therapy are preposterous—the results to be expected, for example, and the ten powers.

Except only what you wish to accept. The list of results to be expected is intended primarily to answer the question, "What is E-Therapy <u>for</u>?" The items listed are widely known consequences of personal integration and many of them have appeared during and after E-Therapy. Certainly the widely known consequences of personal integration in general may be expected by those who take up E-Therapy in particular.

As for the ten powers of E, they have all been observed in prodigies of various sorts and in E-transients in varying degrees of effectiveness. If you doubt the existence of extra-sensory perception in general, it may help you to read 'The Reach of the Mind' by J.B. Rhine. On the other hand, if you have a deep and abiding belief in the rightness of orthodox science, you should carefully read 'The Books of Charles Fort' (published by Holt). You don't have to accept anything in order to progress in E-Therapy, but you should suspend your objections temporarily—at least during the period of therapy.

I doubt that I have an E.

Do you doubt that you have a mind?

Yes I doubt that too.

Why?

Because I've been studying the modern 'operational' school of psychology.

Is this the school which doubts the existence of all things which cannot be observed externally?

Yes. Terms such as 'feeling', 'mind', 'wisdom', 'happiness', etc., Are all considered suspect.

How about the term 'itch'?

Unless a man is observed to scratch himself, we cannot say that he itches.

Have you ever itched without scratching?

Yes.

Is an itch that isn't scratched less real than an itch that is scratched?

No—an itch that isn't scratched is usually more real than one that is scratched.

But doesn't the 'operational' school tend toward the opposite view?

Yes.

Then, are the views of this school realistic? Aren't they <u>false information</u>, and don't they <u>obstruct</u> personal integration rather than produce it?

I strongly believe in psychic phenomena and I am guided by discarnate entities, by spirits.

Can spirits communicate directly with everyone?

No. Few entities are strong enough to communicate with anyone who is not psychically sensitive?

Does one entity ever impersonate another?

Yes, sometimes this will be done—either as a joke or for some serious purpose.

Then let me point out something to you. E is an entity which can communicate with sixty to eighty percent of the population; this means that E is at least a hundred times more powerful than any other communicating entity. Also, we know that in E-Strategy, E can create situations which the transient cannot tell from the real thing, and in these situations E frequently impersonates many persons. E can also produce extraordinary phenomena of many kinds such as turn-off, fire, tremolo, etc. Now the question is—since E is so powerful and so wise and so able, <u>how do we know that all psychic phenomena are not produced by E?</u> In short, if the spirit of your uncle George communicates with you, is it really uncle George or is it your E impersonating your uncle George in order to help you? Can you answer this question?

I think that it is preposterous to speak of recalling early events such as birth or events before birth, and this business of 'former lives' is fantastic and absurd.

Why?

Because of what we know about the structure and growth of the nervous system.

Aren't you assuming the recording of events requires a nervous system?

Why, certainly.

Well, of course, you may be right. It may be that all such apparent recalls are constructed by E for therapeutic purposes, and have no basis in fact. Who can say? On the other hand, the existence of extra-sensory faculties has been accepted by all scientific authorities competent to pass upon the evidence—and this is ever since 1938. (See, 'The Reach of the Mind' by Dr.J.B. Rhine.) Little or nothing is known among scientists about the structural nature of the extra-sensory faculties, and this same vagueness may characterize scientific knowledge about the structural basis of recall. We know far too little about structure, at least in scientific circles, to be able to say with certainty that something is preposterous or absurd.

I am a religious man, and it seems to me that asking for the help of E is the same thing as praying to God. Why shouldn't I just pray to God for what I want?

So far as we know, it is quite accurate to refer to E as the father within, the holy spirit, the comforter, the witness, or the Messiah. If you regard God as an intelligent transforming power within you, praying to God is equivalent to asking E. But if the God to whom you pray is a static picture of belief, you are hampering your E with fixed ideas. Most religious people pray to a God who is remote from them, an abstract product of tradition and belief, and such an inanimate deity is not very effective. A fortunate few, however, pray to a God who is a live wire within, and to such as these the Lord's prayer is an asking of E.

Another point: praying to God for what you want is telling God what to do, and this is against the rules. If you want God's help, ask for, but let God decide what form it will take—unless you think you are wiser than God.

If God is thought of as having the ten powers then E-Therapy is God-Therapy. Will you try it?

I say that you have made extravagant claims that are misleading, and worse, because they will turn the best minds against E-Therapy as a crackpot proposition. The claims <u>may</u> be true, but you will have a difficult time proving it.

In E-Therapy it is E who does the proving; we observers make no effort to persuade. If you are interested in E-Therapy, we will help you, but we have no desire to <u>convert</u> anyone. You must decide for yourself what your attitude will be.

We are inclined to feel that the people who are interested in E-Therapy are motivated by their own Es and do not need to be persuaded. We work for E and for the people E brings us, and those who prefer to live without E-Therapy may have very good reasons for it.

We assume that the 'best minds' you speak of are members of the academic and professional fields who generally prefer a conservative and dignified approach. Such 'best minds' have usually been the last to recognise any true innovation, and we are making no effort to seek their approval. We try to avoid the academic extreme of scepticism and the religious extreme of credulity in telling the truth about E-Therapy as we see it.

I am very happily married, and I'm afraid that E-Therapy may make me less responsive to my husband. I don't want to become too detached.

There isn't anything negative about personal integration; you will never become more integrated than you want to be.

The sexual relationship involves <u>turn-off</u> of the world's irritations, and one's quality of response varies accordingly. The best sexual response is <u>fire</u>, and well integrated persons regard sex as a means to <u>fire</u>. The next best response is <u>tremolo</u>, which is often accompanied by some <u>fire</u>. The next best response is delight in the body and its sexual <u>posturing</u>. Some people find pleasure in the sexual relationship because of the circumstances surrounding it (romance, intrigue, adventure, etc.); they enjoy its place in <u>history</u>. Others respond when sex is successful <u>strategy</u>, *a means to an end, and still others enter into the sexual relationship vindictively, as a form of combat or argument.*

E-Therapy will help you climb this ladder of responses until you are completely fulfilled in them. Your E will show you what is beyond sex when you're ready, but not before.

I'm about to marry a very beautiful woman who is much admired by other men. What I want from E-Therapy is the power to keep her happy with me.

You will get the power you want much more quickly if you do not specifically ask for it. A beautiful woman who has many admirers is most attracted (if she is in good health) to a man who is physically, emotionally, mentally integrated, and of these three qualities the most important is mental integration or insight. The man who has acquired insights sees deeply into people and relationships, and intrigues the lady of beauty because he is not carried away by her power to attract. Such a man is a master of beauty rather than mastered by it. The man who has accumulated understanding is described in "Song of the Answerer" by Walt Whitman, and his power over beauty is described in the "the Fountainhead" by Ayn Rand.

If you give yourself into the hands of your E, and make a special study of E-minus material, you will become the kind of man who need never fear competition, and your wife will achieve happiness which so few beautiful women know how to find.

I don't see how E-Therapy can help me because it is a rigid technique, and I do not think any crystallized technique can benefit the mind.

You apparently are assuming that the three stages and eight factors constitute a technique. They do not; they are simply a catalogue of things E has been observed to do, and could probably be presented in eight stages and seventy-three factors. There is nothing rigid in this catalogue of effects. The only technique in E-therapy is to let E decide what technique to use, and E seems to know them all and use a good many. E-Therapy consists in calling in a therapist who knows exactly what to do—and leaving all choice of method or technique up to him.

These examples of argument and its countering will help the observer to understand the art, and experience in watching Es at work will complete his education. All of this material that is helpful has been learned from various Es; the part that isn't helpful is the contribution of the writers identifications. Whoever can successfully subtract the latter from the former will master the art of E-observing.

E-PLUS

If the transient's E does not appear to be very effective, the observer may ask:

Does E wish me to assist actively?

In an E-Therapy case the answer will be negative, and the observer may practice the virtue of patience. But if the answer is "yes", or if there is no answer, 'E-plus' is required. 'E-plus therapy' is 'E-plus active assistance' therapy. In this therapy the relationship between the transient's E and the observer is like that existing between the director and the assistant director in a motion picture company. Just as the motion picture director makes all vital decisions, while the assistant director does most of the work of managing the company, so in E-plus therapy the transient's E indicates and directs what is to be done, leaving the observer the task of conducting the actual operations. E-plus therapy is therapy in which the observer act as an assistant E, using his own best judgement doing what he has seen Es do.

Thus only experienced E-observers are qualified to do E-plus therapy, and the subject cannot be discussed in detail in such a work as this. Before very long a serviceable E-plus text, containing the findings of many experienced observers, will be available. Nevertheless, certain useful stratagems may be presented here.

If E has asked for such active assistance, the observer may say:

Will E please give me a clue to work on?

E usually answers this request by showing the transient some scene or incident, and the task of the observer is to help the transient obtain a closer understanding of the scene or incident shown. This may be done by asking questions or having the transient repeat some phrase related to the incident, or in one of several other ways. In some cases, the Observer may ask:

What is obstructing the work of E?

E may then indicate in some way what the observer and transient should do in order to make suitable contact with E, and the case then becomes a regular E-case.

One experienced observer (Adams) reports that many transients prevent themselves from entering into therapy by trying too hard to get phenomena and having too strong an attitude of expectancy. This tenseness and rigidity of attitude can indeed be a serious obstacle. In such cases, the observer may say:

Suppose nothing happens in this session—not even any turn-off. Let's even suppose that nothing happens in the next five or six sessions. Will the world come to an end? Won't you go on living just about as usual, just as you have been doing?

This tactic is sufficient in most cases to cause the transient to discard the fixed attitude as ridiculous, and E can proceed with therapy.

Alcoholics and other persons who may not be able to give their attention properly may be helped by the method set forth in Client-Centred Therapy by Dr Carl Rogers; these methods are verbal counselling techniques which may be applied in ordinary conversation. Dr Rogers book is recommended as an authoritative text on many of the factors involved in E-therapy, a thoroughgoing and worth-while book.

Another important E-plus procedure is for the observer to try to 'coach' the transient into turn-off, pointing out that one shouldn't try to make the mind quiet—just let it wander, watching it without approving or disapproving—and it will gradually become quiet. This method is frequently successful.

There is an interesting form of E-plus therapy which may be called 'E-double-plus' or 'hyper-E'. This consists in having the observer's E tell the observer what to do to help a transient achieve contact with his own E.

Sounds miraculous, doesn't it?

Some observers found that they could tell, without looking, when a transient was in turn-off. They didn't know how they knew, but they were always right. Apparently their Es told them.

Some transients can tell whether or not a number is prime (a prime number is one such as 2, 3, 5, 7…..127, 4481 which is not divisible by any other prime number) instantly and without calculating. Apparently their Es tell them.

All these prodigies are powers of E.

Now let a transient who cannot contact his E work with an observer who has good contacts with his E. Can't the transient's E communicate directly with the observer's E? Can't the observer's E tell the observer what to do, or what to tell the transient? Doesn't this amount to indirect contact between the transient and his own E?

That is hyper-E. The difficulty is that observers who have good contact are not yet very numerous.

A still rarer form of E-plus therapy, may be called 'E-triple-plus' or 'fire transmission'. This consists in transmitting fire into a transient who needs it in order to contact his E, for it has been found that persons who have fire in abundance can transmit it to others who lack it. The transient's E can work with fire thus received, and much can be accomplished in a short time. Again persons who have fire in abundance are still comparatively rare.

Nevertheless, there is a natural balance in these matters. The general population can move divided into four classes:

1. Those who can respond to E-Therapy.
2. Those who need E + or assisted-E-Therapy.
3. Those who need E ++ or hyper-E-Therapy.
4. Those who need E+++ or fire-transmission therapy.

Now it so happens that E-Therapy is not difficult to learn; enough people can become E -observers to help all those who can respond to E-therapy. Of these E-observers, a sufficient number can provide E + for all those who need it, a smaller number can provide hyper-E for the smaller number who need it, and a few can provide sufficient fire transmission for the few need it.

What of the recalcitrant husband or wife or parent or child who is hostile to the idea of therapy? A surprisingly large percentage of people seem to feel that they are all right as they are and need no improvement, and some of these are so full of tension that they irritate others. How can one help a child who is too young to understand the idea of a 'magic friend' inside? How can E-Therapy be given to a deaf person, or to a person who is otherwise prevented from entering into a session?

Es have told us how. Let A observe B in an E-session, both asking their Es (and C's E) to let C's tensions and identifications be released through B. B thus acts as a proxy for C. This can be done without C's knowledge, for when C's tensions are sufficiently released, C's E may impel C to express an interest in receiving therapy.

Incredible? Ask those who have tried it.

It is also possible to do this without an observer; B can ask that C's tensions can be transferred to B and there released.

Of course, E-Therapy is impossible (to some), and hyper-E is miraculous. Yet there comes a time when observers can say, "The impossible we do immediately; the miraculous takes a little longer."

E – MINUS

The words 'I am' are potent words;
be careful what you hitch them to.
The thing you're claiming has a way
of reaching back and claiming you!

The removal of identifications is the entire task of E. It is a subject that E knows all about. Nevertheless, the conscious mind can learn much about dis-identifying, and this is a great help. E-minus is the art of conscious dis-identifying, and it is called 'E-minus' because it does not depend upon E at all and can be done by persons in whom E does not manifest.

A certain amount of E-minus information is useful to anyone; Es teach a great deal of it. Pages 47, 48, and 49 contain E-minus information; go back and look at them now.

———————————

Each thing, person, or idea is changeable, uncertain, subject to change without notice; even though some ideas may seem to be permanent, we who think of them do so in changing ways. This is something nobody denies. Yet we habitually identify these changeable, unpredictable factors of life with words and symbols which do not change. This causes a great deal of mischief. It causes us to expect things, people, and ideas to be more stable and reliable than they are capable of being in this changeable world; such expectations are a major cause of conflict and suffering.

Suppose that two variables called 'John' and 'Mary' get 'married'. For a year they complement one another living together in 'pleasant harmony'. Then 'John' flows into a phase called 'alcoholism' and 'Mary' is transformed into 'frigidity';

the relationship called 'pleasant harmony' has ceased to exist. The two variables manifest 'bitterness' and 'resentment'.

Why? 'Pleasant harmony' is guaranteed to no one, yet 'John' and 'Mary' feel that they have been 'betrayed' and 'defrauded'.

The trouble here is that two variables thought they were constants, misled by the constants 'John' and 'Mary', for the names were constant.

Had the two variables fully realized that they were variables, the phases called 'alcoholism' and 'frigidity' might have appeared, but there would have been less 'bitterness' and 'resentment', and this in turn would have resulted in less 'alcoholism' and 'frigidity'.

Misinformation about variableness this is a deadly thing.

Now how can knowledge of this kind help you?

Well, first of all, you see that it is so. You see the suffering that appears in people because they mistakenly thought a variable was a constant.

Secondly, you understand how it works. The entire mechanism of conflict begins to reveal itself to you.

Thirdly, you become better integrated, for conflicts which you understood no longer arise in you.

Fourthly, your mind is improved. As a result of your integration, your faculties are now clear and sharp.

Fifthly, you fully understand, for your insight is now so penetrating that you can help others as well as yourself.

Sixthly, you become fully integrated, and are permanently free from all forms of suffering caused by misinformation about variableness. All the other advantages of full integration are yours to enjoy to use in helping others achieve their integration.

Now, this is not a text in E-minus subject matter; our purpose is only to show what E- minus is. Fortunately, there are some good books available which contain much valuable material, and it is recommended that you make use of them. Certainly there is no field of investigation which will better equip you to be an <u>observer.</u>

Which are the books which contain E-minus information? Some are fiction and some are non-fiction. If you liked Emerson's essays, you can study them. One of the best American sources of É-minus thinking is the book 'Leaves of Grass' by Walt Whitman, also his 'Preface to the 1855 Edition'. A later E-minus writer, especially helpful to persons who take scientific orthodoxy too seriously, was Charles Fort (see 'The Books of Charles Fort', published by Holt). A powerful novel with some E-minus teaching is 'The Fountainhead' by Ayn Rand, and similar messages are to be found in 'Jean-Christophe', by Romain Rowland, and 'The Moon and Sixpence' by Somerset Maugham. Aldous Huxley's 'After Many a Summer Dies the Swan' contains interesting observations, as does 'Hypatia' by Charles Kingsley. Difficult reading, but interesting to some are 'All and Everything' by G. Gurdjieff and 'Science and Sanity' by A. Korzybski.

Socrates was an E-minus therapist, and his more characteristic dialogues are worth consulting, as well as his 'Apology'. Reading 'Flatland' by Edwin Abbott will exercise the E-minus muscles, as well 'The Philosophy of <u>As If</u>' by Vaihinger. Those who like science-fiction will find E-minus thinking in the novels of E. E. Smith and in the 'A' novels of A. E. Van Vogt.

Devotees of the exotic in literature will find E-minus material in 'A Dweller of Two Planets' by 'Phylos' and in 'The

Ninth Vibration', 'The Key of Dreams', 'The Perfume of the Rainbow', 'The Treasure of Ho' and other books by L. Adams Beck. Adventure stories with an E-minus background are 'Tros of Samothrace', ' Black Light', and 'The Devil's Guard' by Talbot Mundy, and 'The Fuse' and 'The World Emperor' by P.B.A.

'A Search in Secret India' by Paul Brunton contains interviews with some E-minus thinkers as does 'God is My Adventure' by Rom Landau. 'Philosophers of India' by Zimmer is a good general text, but the best detailed treatment of the Oriental E-minus teachings is 'The Time Teachers' by P.B.A.

An outstanding teacher of E-minus integration, an Oriental by birth but an Occidental in upbringing, is living at the time of this writing. This man, Jiddu Krishnamurti (1895-1986) has reached the goal that E intends for us (if this writer is any judge), and his extemporaneous talks are very useful to those who can understand them. A publication list can be had from Krishnamurti Writings, Inc., Ojai, California, or, if you're in a hurry, send twenty dollars and ask for 'all the talks'. We know several who have done this, and none of them regret it.

It is has been said that there are three kinds of teachers—worldly, unworldly, and integrative. The worldly teachers are those who accept man as he is in his normal worldly state, and endeavour to work out laws and principles which make orderly living possible—teachers such as Hammurabi, Manu, Moses, Confucius, Machiavelli, Blackstone, Marx, Freud and Emily Post. The unworldly teachers are opposed to the worldly life and seek to interest us in the 'higher' life, favoring fire as opposed to sex, monasticism as opposed to the married state, asceticism as opposed to the pursuit of pleasure and gain, idealism as opposed to agnosticism, mentalism as opposed to materialism, faith as opposed to skepticism, etc. —teachers such as the great mystics and the occultists, Mother Ann Lee, George Fox, Sri Ramakrishna, Sri Chaitanya, Manly Hall and many ministers. The integrative teachers do not take sides in this conflict between the worldly and unworldly elements; they are concerned with the integrative transformation of the individual into a condition that is more spontaneous and less mechanical, more free and less bound—teachers such as Socrates, Whitman, Emerson, Kapila, Krishna, Lao Tzu.... anyone like your E.

Now there are four degrees of integration which are obtainable by E-minus methods, with or without the help of E. The first degree of integration is achieved when one fully understands what full integration is and how to obtain it. Such a person sees the goal and how to reach it, and thereby becomes free from all beliefs, speculations, and opinions about the nature of personal integration. Being free from theories, this person is theoretically free and has the assurance of arriving eventually at practical freedom or full integration, for the attainment is permanent and irreversible; the total amputation of speculative beliefs is no less permanent than any other amputation. This condition of assurance is achieved by an act of understanding or insight or comprehension; there is no work to do other than this.

If the assured person takes up the work of dis-identifying, a second degree of freedom or integration is reached; this involves an emotional integration and lessening of dissipative factors to such an extent that some fire is experienced.

If a twice-freed person proceeds to eliminate all forms of physical dissipation so that fire-experiences may be obtained, the third freedom is reached, a condition devoid of physical identifications.

Finally, if a thrice-freed person proceeds to remove all identifications without remainder and become one who is spontaneous and free from the re-playing of recordings, the condition achieved is full integration. Such a person never again suffers fear, hatred, or grief.

On page 36 four drives are mentioned—those toward

physical fulfilment	(personal),
emotional fulfilment	(relational),
mental fulfilment	(associational), and
ultimate fulfilment	(transcendental).

The fourth of these drives, which causes us to seek out a religion or philosophy, an answer to ultimate questions, is permanently satisfied by the first freedom.

The third of these drives, which causes us to seek out mental companionship in organizations, groups, societies, is permanently satisfied by the second freedom.

The second of these drives, which causes us to seek out emotional companions, lovers, family relationships, stimulants and entertainments, is probably satisfied by the third freedom.

The first of these drives, which causes us to be preoccupied with our own happiness, our own security, and with having our own way, is permanently satisfied by the fourth freedom.

It is possible for <u>you</u> to become fully integrated.

QUALIFICATIONS

Are you a good transient? Are you a good observer? Is E-Therapy a good therapy? Is the writer of these pages qualified to present it ? Has he done a good job?

These are important questions and must be considered carefully.

What must you do to be a good transient?

1. Recognise that your E is not interested in converting you to any fixed 'ism' or belief. If you feel inclined to identify yourself with any exclusive ideology, that is an identification —it is not the intention of your E.

2. Recognise that your E never <u>compels</u> you to do anything; E has no wish to dominate. If you think you are 'commanded' to recite a prayer on a street-corner or commit adultery with a neighbor, that is <u>not</u> your E; <u>E does not command.</u>

3. Recognise that your E does not insist upon a fixed nomenclature or vocabulary; you are at liberty to call E-Therapy itself and the phenomena observed in it by any names you please. If you do not like this writer's method of presenting E-Therapy, use or write your own presentation.

4. Recognize that the process of becoming integrated involves <u>changing</u>; be prepared to change. Your past conditioning shows in your indulgences and irritations; make an effort to avoid both. If one of your indulgences is smoking, for example, cut down on it until you aren't getting much pleasure out of it, but not so much that you are irritated by having so few smokes. This puts you in neutral gear, so to speak, so that transformation is possible. And don't take a free ride in E-Therapy; if you aren't exchanging sessions with someone, pay your observer enough for his time so that you

are not exploiting him, but not so much that he is exploiting you. In all these matters, let your motto be, "neither too much nor too little".

5. Don't try to dominate your E or your observer, and don't expect either of them to dominate you. Be neither authoritative nor subservient. Look upon your E as your companion, guide and friend—and look upon your observer as the friend with whom you visit E.

6. Don't expect your E and your observer to do all the work of integrating you. Observe yourself, your thoughts, words, and actions—without approval or disapproval—constantly, as E does.

What must you do to be a good observer?

1. Never let your pet ideologies intrude into your E-work. No matter how enthusiastic a Rosicrucian, Theosophist, semanticist, sociologist, physical culturist, spiritualist, yogi or commissar you may be, keep it to yourself when in contact with transients. If your conversation before, during and after sessions is full of your opinions and interpretations from (for example) the point of view of a psychic, you are not confident to act as an E-observer. Fully confident E, E +, E ++, and E +++ observers should have obtained the first, second third and fourth degrees of integration (see pages 77 & 78); you should try for the first, at least.

2. In E-Therapy, don't tell E or the transient what to do, and in the E-plus therapies do as little of this as possible.

3. Don't stick to a fixed vocabulary; you and your transients will get tired of any standard nomenclature. It doesn't matter in the least what you <u>call</u> what you do; it is the <u>doing</u> that is important.

4. Don't exploit others, and don't let yourself be exploited. Either exchange your services as an observer for other services, or charge for them—neither too much nor too little.

5. Don't become an ardent admirer of your own intelligence; don't become an ardent admirer of someone else's intelligence. Don't be a leader or a follower, and avoid those persons who expect you to be either.

6. Watch yourself in your work as an observer—look at your motivations and be mindful of them.

Is E-Therapy a good therapy?

1. It has no fixed or exclusive theory or system.

2. It is not a therapy in which one person controls another; the observer does not endanger the transient.

3. No fixed vocabulary or nomenclature is required.

4. It is not an exploitive therapy.

5. It does not proceed from some arbitrary center of authority and orthodoxy; no subservience is required.

6. It is spreading and growing on its merits alone; no salesmanship or propaganda is involved.

Is the writer of these pages qualified to present it?

1. He has achieved the first degree of integration by E-methods (1936), but has not yet responded well as in E-transient (there is some response to E+, E++, and E+++). Thus he is slow in integration.

2. He intends these pages as a letter of introduction; they are not an authoritative text.

3. He recommends the use of a flexible nomenclature.

4. He is anxious neither to exploit nor be exploited.

5. He will accept co-conspirators but not disciples, and expects the same courtesy from others.

6. Having accomplished the task of writing these pages, he refuses to be identified with E-therapy as a movement and is going on to do other things.

Thus this writer is apparently confident enough to prepare this 'letter of introduction', but neither experienced enough nor otherwise qualified to speak on the subject in any authoritative way. In good time we expect more thoroughgoing material from other persons more painstaking.

Nevertheless, even this short 'letter of introduction' contains serious omissions:

Herbert A. Werthauer, in the early days of E-work, observed (it may well be called Werthauer's principle) "let E decide when the session's to end—that is, 'let E end the session when E wishes to do so—and the transient will always feel <u>at</u> <u>least</u> as well as when the session started".

Henry Hill will ask a transient's E, "Can we be finished with this session in sixty minutes?" E usually agrees, and then ends the session exactly at the appointed time. When E does not agree, sessions may last nearly two hours, but Werthauer's principle is seen to work.

The converse of Werthauer's principle is very important. When the transient announces that the session is ended, the observer should ask, "How do you feel?" For if the transient does not feel as well as when the session started, <u>the session is not ended</u>, and the observer must see that the full time needed by E is given.

How is an observer to ask that a session be ended? These words are suitable—

If it is convenient for E to end this session within the next few minutes, we ask that this be done; if it is not convenient, the session may last as long as E wishes.

How often should a transient have sessions? This depends on the type of therapy. It has been found that sessions more often than once in five days may prevent the appearance of fire, as the body needs time to accumulate sufficient energy for fire manifestation. In general, sessions once a week or three times in two weeks seem to bring about integration at a rate which will not be increased by increasing the frequency of sessions.

These statements are valid in a general sense, but the transient's E is the best guide in such matters, or, for that matter, the observer's E.

Some readers have commented that the section on POSTURING is incomplete; mention should have been made of yawning, belching, bicycle-riding motions of the legs, rhythmic poundings of the hands, pelvic writhings, head-twistings and much more. The writer certainly was asleep at the switch when this section was written.

Other readers have objected to the benefits offered in the INVITATION as being too extravagant, especially the comments about 'genius'. The writer wishes to stress that the superconscious mind is the source of all prodigies, just that the conscious mind is the source of all rational undertakings, and the subconscious mind is the origin of all that is irrational. We know a number of persons who have E-sessions for the express purpose of increasing their creative originality in various arts and sciences, and we know of a number of creative accomplishments which are due to E-Therapy.

Some have asked, "What is the legal position of E-observing?" Please read pages 18 and 64. Here it will be seen that E is the power referred to as the 'Messiah', 'Saviour', 'the Father Within', 'the Holy Spirit', the 'Comforter', etc, and it is E who does the therapy, not the observer. Asking E is equivalent to praying (if properly understood), so an E-observer is a person who utters a prayer on behalf of the transient and then sits with the transient to see how the prayer is answered. We do not know of any state or country in which such a practice is illegal, whether paid for or not. An interesting story of remarkable E-Therapy is 'There Is A River' by Thomas Sugrue which tells of Edgar Cayce and his extraordinary E-manifestations.

Some have asked, "How can we help the insane?" Use the method described on page 71—the proxy method. No court or medical authority will ever objected to the treatment of confined persons in this way, for no court or medical authority is likely to consider even the possibility of proxy therapy. It isn't even necessary for the observer or proxy-transient to visit the confined person, although it may help in some cases.

Many have wondered about the applications of the superconscious mind to questions other than those of personal integration. We are not in a position to say much about this yet, except that if the ten powers of E can be made available to the human race in all the ways that are already observed in individuals, all the troubles of the present day will be left far behind. To a small child, an adult seems virtually omniscient. To an average adult, an E-integrated transient will seem so.

An Institute of Integration has been formed to be of service to all persons interested in personal integration and its applications. If you wish to keep up with developments in this field, send a dollar or more to the Institute and you will receive a journal called 'the Integrator'. In the pages of this journal you will learn about lectures, recorded on tape or wire, which are available from the Institute.

For those who respond to it, nothing yet discovered seems better than E-Therapy as described in these pages. But for those who do not respond, promising new E-plus methods have been developed. An excellent method for the beginners is 'group-E', for which we are indebted to Junius Adams of San Francisco. 'Teamed hyper-E' was discovered and developed by the friends and family of Edward Robles in Fair Oaks, California, and the writer has trained large groups in the use of this powerful therapy

'Proxy therapy' (see page 71) was discovered by many persons independently, and it has been demonstrated, by means of electrical instruments, that the tensions of one person _can_ be transferred to another person and there released. 'Insane' persons have been treated with proxy e-therapy, and, strange as it may seem, this remarkable power is actually being considered as a remote-control way of removing the emotional and psychological tensions which cause war!

The writer has developed 'E-minus' into a definite therapy which seems helpful to many, and has come forward with a new method call 'E-Suggestion' or ES-therapy, which consists in using the power of suggestion for the one purpose of improving the transient's response to E. This therapy shows promise of producing talents like those of the late Edgar Cayce.

The Institute is making a systematic study of 'psycho-chemistry', which is concerned with the fact that certain vitamins, endocrine extracts, alkaloids and other chemicals are very helpful in slow cases. With all these new methods, there will be no more 'slow' cases, so that access to 'E' will be available for all.

A primary centre of integrative study and work is being planned by the Institute, as well as subsidiary centers in various city areas throughout the world. With E's help, what can be done will be done.

This book is copyrighted in the United States and internationally by the Institute of Integration (1953).

Publishers note: between 1951-53 various editions of this book were published with slightly different endings one of which we present below.

In a previous drafting of this text, it was reported as follows:

An Institute of Integration was founded to be of service to those interested in integration and its applications.

Anyone who can demonstrate that they have reached the first level of integration (see page 77), can become director of this organization.

If you want to know whether or not you have achieved the first level of integration, please send the Institute your answers to the following questions:

1 - What must be known, including in general?

2 - What needs to be carefully checked ?

3 - What should be rejected, eradicated and renounced in me?

4 - What needs to be achieved, experienced, accomplished?

5 - On which issues do you have to work, what needs to be practiced, developed?

Answer these questions as widely as you think necessary and appropriate, and your answers will be examined by an accredited person.

Want to take part in an important experiment?

There are numbers called Mersenne numbers that have a great interest to mathematicians.

Some of these numbers are prime numbers (see page 70), others are not. Determine if a certain Mersenne number is a prime number or not is something that goes beyond the possibilities of modern science . Your E, can do it? If you have good communication with your E, send us your findings about Mersenne numbers.

M2 = 2^2-1 = 3, prime number

M3 = 2^3 - 1 = 7, prime number

M5 = 2^5 - 1 = 31, prime number

M7 = 2^7 - 1 = 127, prime number

M11 = 2^{11}-1 = 2047 = 23 x 89

M13 = 2^{13}-1 = 8191

M17 = 2^{17}-1

M19 = 2^{19}-1 and so on. We're interested in the numbers of Mersenne M13, M17, M19, 23, 29, 31, 37,41, 43, 47, 53, 59, 61, 67, 71, 73, 79, 83, 89, 97, 101, 103, 107, 109, 113, 127, 131, 137, 139, 149, 151, 157, 163, 167, 173, 179, 181, 191, 193, 197, 199, 211, 223, 227, 229, and so on. (All numbers listed are prime numbers)

If your E can tell you that M8191 is a prime number, or that has the factor of 599 (just as an example), we can examine your answers and tell you whether (with the help of your E) you have done something beyond the scope of modern science and the ability of any electronic brain. (M8191, for example, is composed of 2466 numbers). If you want the world to recognize the powers of E quickly, please help in this experiment.

Los Angeles, January 1952

Alva la Salle 'Beau' Kitselman age 22, at Stanford University

A. L. Kitselman

E-Therapy

INSTITUTE OF INTEGRATION

THIRTY EAST SIXTIETH STREET

NEW YORK CITY

E-Therapy — original

INVITATION

Would you like to improve your conduct? Is there a habit you'd like to get rid of?

Would you like to experience extreme physical pleasure? Intense, ever-fresh happiness? Deep, impartial calmness?

Would you like to lose the feeling of insecurity? Make an end of doubt and perplexity? Lose all sense of fear, hatred, and grief?

Would you like to become a prodigy in science, government, business, art or education? A genius in originality, mental grasp, or in understanding others? Would you like to develop supernormal powers?

Would you like to become fully integrated? To be directly aware of things (without needing to sense them or think about them)? To realize a state of being in which there is no obstruction?

These pages tell how. They tell of E-Therapy, which is the simplest and most effective method of personal integration known to me at this time.

A. L. Kitselman

APPROACH

Greatness exists in every person who can recognize greatness. He who composes, and he who appreciates, a great symphony are equally great in appreciation; the difference is only that the composer can construct what both can appreciate. Greatness is passive in both, while active in only the composer. All persons who fully appreciate a great work of art are potentially as great as the maker thereof.

So also with works of literature, science and philosophy. He who can admire a revolutionary mathematical proof is potentially as great as the originator thereof. All who can find delight in the works of Whitman, Newton, or Emerson are potential Whitmans, Newtons, or Emersons.

The problem is how to transform the potential into the actual. Greatness is in us; how can we let it out?

It is the purpose of these pages to show that greatness can let itself out; it needs only to be asked. It is no exaggeration to say that both the method and its results are little short of miraculous.

2

What is this method?

It can take a thousand forms. One extremely simple approach is for one person to say to another, "Let us ask your mind to take whatever steps are necessary in order to remove whatever is obstructing it. Relax, close your eyes, and let's see what happens."

In some cases such a procedure will bring results never experienced before — such interesting results as have been mentioned.

Two conditions seem to be essential:

a. There must be a request for action, and

b. The transient (the person experiencing the process of transformation) must passively watch what happens.

This second condition seems to be helped in most cases by having another person present to make the request and to watch how things go, so that the transient will remain passive and attentive. This other person seems to act as an energizing observer, so to speak, and may be called the 'observer'.

The experiment conducted by transient and observer is called a 'session', and may last a few minutes or a few hours. Sessions are usually about one hour long.

3

Now, that part of the mind which removes obstructions may be called by any name the transient prefers. It has been called the 'examiner', the 'integrator', the 'purifier', the 'decontaminator', the 'master', the 'observer', the 'fellow inside', the 'natural clearing mechanism', the 'great one', the 'wise man', the 'inner voice', the 'witness', the 'perfect one', the 'saviour', the 'messiah', the 'redeemer', the 'ideal', the 'Lord', the 'sage', 'Sri Krishna', the 'pure one', the 'protector', the 'teacher', the 'integral', the 'omniscient', the 'holy spirit', the 'comforter', the 'buddha', the 'over-soul', the 'higher self', the 'super-mind', the 'super-ego', the 'ultra-mind', the 'transformer', the 'all-knowing', the 'buddhi', the 'prajña', the 'bodhi', the 'aumakua', 'something tells me', 'I've got a hunch', and 'Rover'. Since the name to be used depends upon the transient, we shall write "E" whenever this part of the mind is meant, and the proper word is to be verbally filled in.

An E-Therapy session, then, consists of a _transient_ with a certain _knowledge_ of E an _observer_ with a certain _knowledge_ of E and _work_ done by E; five factors are involved.

What can E-Therapy accomplish, and how long does it take? The list of possible accomplishments has already been given (see Invitation), and the length of time required to bring about a desired change depends upon the five factors just mentioned. If transient and observer are both in good health, and each has a good understanding of E, then spectacular results may be expected within a few hours.

The case of Mrs. C. P. is an illustration of this. In August of 1950 she was depressed and irritable as a consequence of going back to college at age 35 while trying to cook, wash, and keep house for her husband and two young daughters. Her college work was extremely difficult for her as she had forgotten how to study. She was unable to take part in a required swimming course because of a deathly fear of water. Despite all her efforts she was failing in her studies, and she became so irritated with her children that she frequently found herself yelling at them.

At this point her husband repeated a one-paragraph invitation to E (which he had just heard over the telephone) and she went into a one-hour E-session which was accompanied by a feeling of extreme physical and emotional well-being. Since this first session she has enjoyed such remarkable emotional richness that she frequently feels the skin-tingling thrills and flashes of ecstasy which most people experience only in their youth. In the eyes of her friends she lost five or ten years, both in appearance and manner. This one session ended her depression and reduced her irritability to such a point that she found herself yelling at her daughters not more than once a week. Nevertheless, she still had difficulty with her studies, as before. At intervals of five days she was given five more one-hour sessions, and her grades have moved from the B-C-D range to the A-B range. Whereas formerly she used to study slowly and laboriously, reading with poor comprehension, making many notes and painstakingly memorizing them, she now reads quickly and easily, makes no notes, and memorizes nothing. When examination time comes, she attends without special preparation, mentally calls upon E to help her, and finds that she can answer any question instantly _if she has read the answer at any time_. She has lost her fear of water and is the star of her swimming class. She got one degree with such ease that she is continuing her studies in order to get another. Six hours of E did this.

6

As to what this miracle-working E really is, it is important to learn this from experience rather than make theories about it. There seems to be an endless variety of such experiences, as well as an endless variety of theories about E. The ordinary mind seems to deal with specific things in a simple, step-by-step way, while E appears to handle whole groups of things simultaneously and in a manner that is both subtle and wondrous. The ordinary mind is full of opinions, motives, and compulsions and has limited fields of interest and action; E is not conditioned or compelled in any way and does not seem to be interested in limited fields or abilities. The ordinary mind and E co-operate in us, although they are different in character. The nature of this co-operation is something to think about, and what this particular kind of thinking does to us is also something to think about, for it is the gateway to all that is wonderful.

7

ASKING

Why is it that E will help a transient when asked to do so? Why is it necessary to ask? If E has the power to help, why doesn't he help without being asked? If E has always dwelt within us, why aren't we perfect already? If there is really a miraculous transforming intelligence within us, why weren't we all perfect years ago? If E has done nothing for us up till now, why start now? Isn't this whole business rather ridiculous?

Suppose that your next-door neighbor was a wise man. Unless you had wisdom yourself, you wouldn't know that your neighbor was wise. He would make no effort to tell you about his wisdom, for conceit is not a part of wisdom. He would not be interested in showing you the error of your ways, for he would be free from the missionary impulse. Though he might have many wondrous powers, they would be invisible to you. You might easily live next door to such a man for ten, twenty, or thirty years without ever suspecting anything out of the ordinary.

8

Suppose something threatened you in some way. Your wise neighbor might easily protect you with his wisdom, but would you realize that he had done so? It isn't likely. Even in times of calamity you might be helped without knowing it, for wisdom does not advertise itself. How, then, would you ever find out that your neighbor was wise?

Only by asking. Ask a wise man to help you understand yourself, and he is at your service instantly, for self-knowledge is the beginning of wisdom. Ask him about anything else and he will ask you why you want to know, thus directing you back to the task of understanding yourself. Only on rare occasions will he discuss any other subject.

Of course, few of us have a wise man living next door, pleasant though that might be. All of happiness might come from such an association. Yet in each of us there is a wise man who lives much closer than next door, as wise as the wisest man who ever lived, as wise as wisdom itself. We call this wise man within us "E", and we say that E is that part of our own mind which is clear and wise. But who knows what E is? Perhaps only E _knows_

9

we can make theories. E is important, however, that we have either no theory or several; to have <u>one</u> theory is to pretend to know. Theory or no theory, E does do a great many things, and it is useful to know what E can do.

Now we can answer the questions with which we started. E will help a transient when asked to do so because a transient is a seeker of self-understanding. It is necessary to ask because E has no desire to interfere with the transient's independence. E doesn't help without being asked, except in an emergency and secretly, because it is important for us to use such intelligence as we have. Though E has always dwelt in us, we are not thereby made perfect because it has not previously occurred to us that perfection is either possible or practicable. Although there really <u>is</u> a miraculous transforming power within us, we were not perfect years ago because we didn't know about E or what E can do. Though E may have done no recognizable wonders for us to-date, E will start now because we are asking it; we are asking for self-understanding <u>now</u>. And, finally, for these and other reasons it is decidedly <u>not</u> correct to say that this whole business is ridiculous. E-Therapy is something that <u>works</u>.

How, then, does it work? How does one become a _transient_, or an _observer_?

Reading these pages will turn a _static_ or inert personality into a _transient_ or changing personality, for whoever reads these pages must give _some_ thought to E, and E responds to the slightest touch.

There are many, however, who cannot read these words. How are they to be helped? How does one act as an _observer_?

To act as an observer, let the candidate for E-transformation read this material, or tell the substance of it in your own words. See that your candidate understands the general idea of a subconscious mind which is inferior to the conscious mind, and a superconscious mind which is superior to the conscious mind. An anecdote or a question about mistaken identifications (such as the poverty-bred idea that being rich equals happiness) will serve to illustrate the subconscious mind, while a super-normal mental phenomenon (such as the unconscious solving of problems or the ability of a mental prodigy) will illustrate the superconscious.

This general introductory material should be presented simply and without argument. When you discuss the subconscious, don't talk about the theories of Mesmer, Braid, Freud, Jung, etc., and when you mention the superconscious, don't talk about the theories of Rhine, Hubbard, Kitselman, Werthauer, Altman, Fisher, etc. And don't talk about your own pet theories, either. Theories have no place in this preliminary discussion; let your measure of what is acceptable be Whitman's maxim, "Only what nobody denies, is so."

This means that you must avoid positive and unsupported statements, most of which cause instant controversy. Suppose you start out by announcing authoritatively, "Freud discovered the subconscious mind; Kitselman discovered the superconscious mind." An uninformed person will be entirely unimpressed, never having heard of either man or either mind. An average person will be intimidated by your statement and attitude; this will be a barrier between you. An informed person will classify you as a nincompoop because neither announcement is true except in a limited frame of reference, and because, even in that familiar area, many other heads were involved in each discovery.

12

Furthermore, don't claim that the three minds are a unit (or that they aren't); some people are greatly disturbed by such over-simplifications. And don't talk about the views of the Theosophists, Rosicrucians, Anthroposophists, etc. If the views of these groups were helpful in achieving personal integration, we would all have become Theosophists, Rosicrucians, or Anthroposophists long ago. The simple fact is that personal integration does not depend on any thesis that there is (or there is not) life after death, or that things are (or are not) predetermined, or that virtue is (or is not) rewarded. Personal integration is to be _experienced_, not believed in; kindly leave beliefs out of discussion.

If you like, you can compare the subconscious, conscious, and superconscious to the spectrum of light — infra-red, visible, & ultra-violet —. This is a handy way of straddling the question of whether they are one, or three. The thing to remember is that your transient _must_ understand something about what goes on in E-Therapy. Your job in this preliminary discussion is to provide this understanding without raising _any_ points of controversy.

Here is a practical example of asking:

Have you ever had the experience of suddenly understanding something about yourself that you had never understood before?

Oh, yes — many times, I suppose.

Did you ever discover that one of your personal actions or attitudes actually had its origin in some silly misconception?

Yes, I did. For years I had a guilty feeling each time I went past an electric power house. One day I realized that I had been gruffly ordered off the premises of a power station when I was just a little boy. Now power stations don't bother me at all.

That's an excellent example of the sort of thing we are concerned with in E-Therapy.

You mean that your whole purpose is just to get rid of misconceptions?

Yes. All we want to do is to get rid of the many mistaken identifications which exist in your mind. As we see it, each identification removed will make you feel just that much better.

Well, its certainly true that I felt guilty near power houses because I still identified power houses with an angry, accusing voice. And its also true that the guilty feelings disappeared as soon as I saw the light — that is, as soon as I saw how silly the identification was and thus removed it. But aren't we normally unconscious of our identifications? How do you propose to get at mine?

The same way you did.

The same way I did? What do you mean? All I did was suddenly realize that something was silly — or is that all I did?

What else do you _think_ you did? Why did you have a sudden realization on that particular day?

I don't know. I suppose I began wondering why power stations upset me, and then, all of a sudden, I _knew_ why.

Had you ever before wondered why power stations disturbed you?

Now that I come to think of it, I never had — I had just accepted that they _did_.

What made you think of the childhood incident which originally caused your misconception?

Ah, that's the _real_ mystery! I had completely forgotten the incident — hadn't thought of it in years, in fact. I've often wondered why I happened to remember that particular incident at that particular time — just when I needed it.

Yes, that's the mystery which led to the discovery of E-Therapy. There seems to be a part of the mind which has the power to remove identifications. It was this part of your mind which caused you to wonder why power stations disturbed you, and then obligingly furnished the answer.

That seems remarkable, if there really is such a power in the mind.

Well, you'll soon be able to find out for yourself about that, because "E-Therapy" is just a name for the work that power does. We think that there is an intelligent power within you which can transform you by removing identifications, and we call this power "E", or whatever name you prefer.

Certainly, if there is any such power in man, it should be called "the Redeemer" or "the Saviour" or some such great name. However, "E" is good enough for me.

All right, then, "E" it is. "E" is our name for the intelligent transforming power within you, and "E-Therapy" is the work E does. Would you like to start now, and let E go to work?

I'm willing. What am I supposed to do?

Lie down, close your eyes, and just watch to see what E will do.

16

Now, some conversation such as the foregoing is all that is necessary to start an E-session. The observer will find information on the various activities of E in the sections which follow, and to which these remarks are an index:

If the transient reports a lessening of some tension or activity in the mind, refer to the section entitled TURN-OFF.

If an especially pleasant feeling or experience is reported, refer to the section on FIRE.

If a more-or-less violent agitation of the body or sense-impressions is experienced, refer to TREMOLO.

If changing postures, body motions or facial grimacing is observed, refer to the POSTURING section.

If incidents are remembered or recalled either fragmentarily or in complete detail, refer to HISTORY.

If a situation is presented in which the transient is apparently expected to do something, refer to the section on STRATEGY.

If the transient says "Why doesn't E start working?" or voices any other criticism or objection, refer to the section entitled ARGUMENT.

If E communicates only rarely and is unable to do much, study the E-PLUS section.

If E seems unable to operate in any way, study the section on E-MINUS.

It may be well to point out here that each and every action of E which is discussed in these pages has been observed in transients who did not know what to expect. E is the one who originated E-Therapy; Kitselman, Nowell, Patnoude, Murphy, Werthauer, Schuman, Altman, & Pinsker are simply the eight first observers of what E can do, the word "first" here meaning only "in the limited frame of reference attendant upon the apparent discovery by Kitselman (observer) and Nowell (transient) on August 28, 1950 in Honolulu". We have learned since that E has been discovered many times before, an excellent example of observer-less E-Therapy being found in the book "I Say Sunrise" by Talbot Mundy, who _died_ several years _before_ Kitselman and Nowell made their 'discovery'. Other clear examples have formulated some aspect of E-Therapy — one as far back as 1250 B.C. Nevertheless, it is doubtful that the present widespread interest (scores of thousands of persons) has been seen before within historical times.

E-Therapy, then, is not the product of suggestion; everything E does will appear in some transient sooner or later, whether suggested or not. Yet it may appear _sooner_ if the transient knows about it.

For this reason it is in order to explain the powers of E to the transient. The example we have given of asking might then conclude as follows:

········· Would you like to start now, and let E go to work?

Won't you tell me, first, just what sort of things I can expect to happen?

Certainly. We have observed ten powers in E. They appear in people whether we tell about them or not, but it is sometimes helpful to know something about them.

First is the power to recognize causes. What motives never lead to a pleasant consequence? What motives never lead to a painful consequence? What are the consequences of thinking something is permanent? What are the consequences of thinking some one thing, person or idea is happiness? What are the effects of identifying with something, of having definite ideas about the 'self'? What are the consequences of removing fixed identifications about permanence, happiness, and the 'self'? What is the effect of fixed opinion? E is equipped with a full understanding of these matters, and can make it clear to you.

Second is the power to judge actions. What is the effect of dissipation? What follows the struggle to get rich? What is the consequence of seeking power over others? What is the result of striving for a reputation? What are the after-effects of killing, stealing, sexual misconduct, dishonesty, slandering others, and so on? E has an understanding of actions and their effects, and can communicate it to you.

Third is the power to measure behavior patterns. What is the effect of banking as a mode of life? If a man is a preacher, what will it do to him? What is the effect of conventional domesticity? What are the consequences of becoming a Trappist, a politician, a juggler, a communist, or a dress-designer? E knows all this, and can tell you.

Fourth is the power to understand structure. What is the person? What factors compose it? What is the exact structure of the body? What are feelings? What is memory? What are motives? What is consciousness? What is matter? What is life? What is its origin? What is its goal? It may seem hard to believe, but E seems to know the answers to all these questions, and can use them to straighten out any structural difficulty.

Fifth is the power of insight into character. How many kinds of people are there? How do they differ? What kind of person is this? Can he or she be trusted? Will this person get along with that person? In addition to knowing these things, E knows all facets of your character and can bring them into proper harmony.

Sixth is the power to measure tendencies. Which are the forces which change a person? How can this tendency be weakened, and that one strengthened? Is this person's character improving or degenerating? How can a man or woman be induced to change for the better? E knows all this, and will proceed to regulate your tendencies for best results.

Seventh is the power to produce attainments. What extraordinary experiences are possible for a person? What are the various levels of understanding? What are the degrees of emotional integration? How can pure ecstatic pleasure be experienced? What is ecstatic happiness, and how can it be reached? Is there such a thing as ecstatic calmness? Can one achieve permanent freedom from perplexity, fear, conceit, and grief? E knows all about these attainments and can cause you to experience them.

21

Eighth is the power to investigate history. What were you doing on August 28, 1950? What was your birth like? What happened during the first year of your life? Did your father and mother fight before you were born? Did you ever live before? All this E knows and can show you in various ways.

Ninth is the power of extra-sensory perception. It has been found repeatedly that one E can communicate with another —and this to so perfect a degree that it is difficult to decide whether there are many Es, or just one. Your E can communicate with my E, apparently, and this may help us in our work. E can also show you many things which have never been apparent to your senses.

Tenth is the power of infallibility. How well you can communicate with your E seems to depend on you, but, subject only to that one limitation, everything E does is right. No E has been known to make a mistake. E has no fear, no conceit, no ignorance, and no carelessness that we can detect.

If you are willing to ask E to help you, just lie down, close your eyes, relax, and watch these ten powers in action!

TURN-OFF

If some tension or activity of the mind seems to be suspended for the time being, this is what is called turn-off. After _asking_ has been completed, the observer should wait three or four minutes. Then, if nothing has been announced by the transient, the observer may ask

What seems to be happening?

If the transient's answer is like one of these:

Nothing seems to be happening.

I can't think of a thing.

My mind is a complete blank.

The worrying I've been doing has suddenly stopped.

There doesn't seem to be _anything_ going on.

My, this is restful!

I've never seen my mind so quiet.

How peaceful it is!

then E is using turn-off, and the observer may make some remarks such as the following:

You appear to be experiencing what we call turn-off. It is as if E has _turned_ off the normal flow of mental impressions. Most E-sessions begin with this turn-off, which normally lasts five or ten minutes or more. Turn-off is often our first evidence of the power of E, because very few people can achieve this condition without the help of E. The fact that you are experiencing it indicates that your E can communicate, and that your case is well under way, for many persons have received great benefit from turn-off alone.

As to why E makes use of this turn-off, it may be that E likes to start with a clean slate, so to speak, and thus wipes the mind clean of all preoccupations before going further. Or it may be that the energy ordinarily consumed in the flow of mental impressions is now being saved up, in order to show you something later on. Or it may be that this is what you are like when the most active and intelligent part of your mind is busy elsewhere — that is, outside your range of consciousness. Any one or all of these explanations may be the true state of affairs; we do not know.

In any event, turn-off is comfortable and good for you. Enjoy it as long as E permits, even if it lasts through the entire session. Do not be impatient for something else to happen; turn-off alone is miracle enough. And don't worry about me; during long waits my E frequently puts me into turn-off along with my transient. Just take it easy.

24

At exactly the right time E will end the turn-off
and proceed to something else. Until then, relax
and enjoy what you are now experiencing.

Although turn-off is apparently one single state
of being, E has the power to turn off (and on again)
many different conditions of the mind. Turn-off may
be momentary (as during part of a session), temporary (lasting an entire session or for a few days or
weeks), or permanent (this involves E-minus attainments). In E-sessions the following processes have
been turned off:

pleasure-craving (for tobacco, alcohol, sex, etc.)
annoyance (anger, hatred, antagonism, etc.)
mental inertia (slowness of mind, mental sluggishness, etc.)
distraction (excitement, worry, fear, panic, etc.)
perplexity (doubt, indecision, uncertainty, etc.)
ignorance (obtuseness, stupidity, confusion, etc.)
boredom (apathy, ennui, etc.)
pain (physical, bodily pain is meant here)
thinking (inquiring and willing)
ecstasy (physiological; see the FIRE section)
happiness (mental, emotional, aesthetic, etc.)
perception of appearances, resistances, diversity
awareness of space

25

awareness of awareness
awareness of 'nothing'
awareness of 'not being aware'
(Some of these may sound strange, but they do
occur, and you may encounter them.)
permanence-identifications (this is permanent)
happiness-identifications (this is happiness)
self-identifications (this is the self, it is mine, etc.)
delighting in something
wanting something
pursuing something
taking up some pursuit
material-identifications (this is substantial, material, solid)
ambition-identifications (strain and strive for this)
security-identifications (this is safe, constant, reliable)
object-interest (this object is interesting, curious, etc.)
motivation (this is the real purpose, motive, aim, etc.)
object-acceptance (this object is real, important, essential)
truth-acceptance (this is the final, certain truth)
delusion-acceptance (false ideas of reality)
protection-acceptance (here I am safe from danger)
over-simplification (thoroughness is not necessary here)
bondage-acceptance (I want to suffer and be limited)
ideological fixations and effects (conditions, motives and
tensions which result from adopting a fixed theory of reality)

Now what are ideological fixations? Are they such widespread and current ideologies as fascism, communism, socialism, capitalism, etc? Yes, of course — but these are only secondary ideologies. The basic ideological fixations are over-simplified views of reality which are arrived at by disregarding whole areas of observation — speculative beliefs such as occultism, materialism, determinism, agnosticism, mentalism, theism, atheism, sectarianism, survivalism, and racism. E seems to take the position that any one of these extreme opinions will cause inflexibility of mind and obstruct the process of integration.

If you are more interested in your beliefs than you are in becoming integrated, it will be best for you to stop at this point, for uncritically accepted beliefs are a bar to personal integration. It will not be possible for you to become a fully integrated communist, fascist, capitalist, or sectarian; fully integrated persons cannot be described with such labels. The best thing to do is to recognize your beliefs as speculations and postpone definitely accepting or rejecting them until you are fully integrated, for surely you will be able to decide more effectively then.

FIRE

If the transient reports
I feel a pleasant tingling accompanied by ecstatic thrills and flashes. It moves through me in waves and there are jolts of pure ecstatic energy in it. I am full of it; I feel it in every cell.
or any portion thereof, or
I see something very beautiful
or hear, feel, perceive, sense, know etc., or
I feel something very strongly. *(neutral or pleasant)*
then the observer may conclude that E is using what is known as fire, *and may say*

Your E has the power to bring you certain intensifications of feeling which are very beneficial. These experiences are sometimes startlingly vivid, but never are harmful. Relax and enjoy what you are experiencing, for it will do you much good.

The word 'fire' is used in this connection because it has been used for a long time to indicate strong feelings or emotional intensity. Thus we speak of 'playing with fire', 'the fire of passion', being 'fired with enthusiasm', being a 'spitfire' or a 'firebrand'; there are similar idioms in ancient Sanskrit, Chinese and Pali.

Ecstatic fire involves physiological ecstasy which may appear in one or several or all of five forms:

skin tingling ('with 'goose bumps', body hair on end, etc.)

thrills or flashes

waves

jolts or tremors (feelings of 'levitating force', etc.)

saturation ('a non-sexual orgasm in every cell')

Tranquil fire is not accompanied by physical ecstasy; it features a quiet sense of happiness. The pleasant feeling in tranquil fire is mental, rather than physical.

Neutral fire contains neither ecstasy nor happiness; it is an intensified feeling of poised neutrality between pleasure and pain, happiness and unhappiness.

Ecstatic fire is apparently the antidote for pain; within certain limits, a transient experiencing ecstatic fire cannot at the same time experience physical pain, a pinch being felt only as pressure, and so on. When ecstatic fire is accompanied by turn-off of inquiring and willing, it is impossible to experience unhappiness. E has been observed to relieve and remove pain and unhappiness by 'turning on' ecstatic fire, and the urge to dissipate is reduced in those who have access to ecstasy, for it is itself the most intense of all physical pleasures.

Pleasure and pleasure-craving are transcended by tranquil fire, for it is the experience of intense happiness without need of pleasure. E has been observed to relieve and remove excess pleasure-craving by 'turning on' tranquil fire.

Transients who progress so far as to experience much tranquil fire may become too preoccupied with their new-found happiness, and neutral fire is a remedy for this, for it is the experience of intense awareness without need for happiness.

It is interesting to observe how thoroughly E provides for the emotional integration of the transient. It has been said that we are mentally and emotionally controlled by four drives — those toward

physical fulfilment   (personal),
emotional fulfilment   (relational),
mental fulfilment   (associational), and
ultimate fulfilment   (transcendental). Now
the emotional realization of these goals is to be found in four principal kinds of fire which E seems inclined to produce in every transient who enjoys good neuro-endocrine health. The mental attainment of these four goals will be discussed in the E-MINUS section; here we are concerned with the four kinds of fire.

What are the four fires?

The first is ecstatic fire associated with thinking (inquiring & willing), and it contains the four factors _thinking_, _ecstasy_, _happiness_ & _intensity_.

The second is ecstatic fire with thinking turned off, and it contains the three factors _ecstasy_, _happiness_ & _intensity_.

The third is tranquil fire, and it contains the two factors _happiness_ & _intensity_.

The fourth is neutral fire, and it contains the two factors _neutrality_ & _intensity_.

How do these four fires fulfill the four drives?

The first fire makes plain, everyday living seem a great adventure, for it involves turn-off of pleasure-craving, annoyance, mental inertia, distraction, perplexity, ignorance, boredom and pain.

The second fire is the heart of ecstasy, all thinking and unhappiness being turned off.

The third fire is the heart of happiness, for it does not contain the comparative grossness of pleasure.

The fourth fire is the heart of poised balance, for it is free from even the comparative grossness of being happy. It has another important quality, for it is said that the state of well-integrated emotional balance is the basis of true objectivity and permits knowing and seeing things as they really are.

Thus the first drive (toward physical fulfilment) is satisfied by the first fire, which is a condition of ecstatic living and thinking.

The second drive (toward emotional fulfilment) is satisfied by the second fire, which is a condition of pure ecstatic pleasure.

The third drive (toward mental fulfilment) is satisfied by the third fire, which is pure happiness.

The fourth drive (toward ultimate fulfilment) is satisfied by the fourth fire, which is pure awareness.

It must be understood that fire is not always at full intensity; sometimes it is quite weak. Fire and turn-off always appear together; there is no fire without turn-off, and there is no turn-off without at least some fire. This is so because turning off any one activity of the mind causes an intensification of the remaining activities, and intensification is a synonym for fire. Thus when a condition opposed to fire is turned off, a complementary condition favorable to fire is turned on. In the preceding section we discussed some of the activities which E can turn off; in this section we are discussing some of the activities which E can turn on. If a transient doesn't like the word 'fire', replace it with 'intensity' or 'turn-on'.

32

In order to correct certain conditions of emotional inhibition, E has been observed to turn on four fire-purified attitudes toward living beings.

The first pure attitude is simple affection, which is equivalent to what is meant by the word 'love' when thought of as distinct from pleasure-desire and possessiveness.

The second pure attitude is compassion, which is genuine concern for those in trouble.

The third pure attitude is sympathy, which is rejoicing in the accomplishments of others.

The fourth pure attitude is neutrality, which is regard for the independence of others.

These four attitudes involve some degree of fire — the first three being forms of the first fire, and the fourth being an aspect of the fourth fire. In a given transient, E may turn them on as directed toward one, several, or many persons — even toward humanity in general. This may also apply to one, several, or many animals — or even toward an entire species, depending on the nature of the case. E uses the four attitudes in helping many, but they are especially powerful instruments in the task of helping repressed and unsympathetic persons.

In some sessions E has shown the transient beautiful colors, such as a beautiful blue color, etc. Some transients have seen beautiful scenes and pictures, heard beautiful sounds or music, tasted wonderful flavors, smelled pleasant odors or perfumes, felt pleasant touch sensations, or thought beautiful thoughts. Such experiences, of course, are all forms of the first fire.

In E-sessions the following processes have been turned on:

dispassion (physical contentment)
the pure attitudes
'lighting up' of the mind (brilliance, clarity)
calmness (imperturbability)
examination (study, scrutiny, evaluation)
understanding (penetration, insight, knowing)
delight (interestedness, enthusiasm, joy)
the four fires
awareness of space
awareness of awareness
awareness of 'nothing'
awareness of 'not being aware'
suspension of feeling and awareness (total turn-off)
(The four awarenesses mentioned above are four abstract fire states related to the fourth fire.)

34

insight into impermanence (changeableness, flux)
insight into unhappiness (being controlled by identification
insight into non-identity (dis-claiming, dis-identifying)
insight into weariness (of being subject to limitations)
insight into dispassion (the basis of fire)
insight into ending (identifications, unhappiness, pain)
insight into releasing (getting free from controls)
insight into crumbling (of all ~~supposed~~ solid realities)
insight into futility (of all specific purposes)
insight into insecurity (nothing is safe, constant, or reliable,
insight into no-object (objects are of secondary importance,
insight into motivelessness (it is spontaneity & creativeness)
insight into emptiness (no preoccupation is worth-while)
insight into transcending (no doctrine is final truth)
knowledge & vision of things as they are (freedom from delusions)
insight into danger (no place or ~~position~~ is ~~safe~~)
insight into caution (one must be ~~thorough~~)
insight into removing (how to get rid of controls)
four attainments of permanent freedom from ideologica
fixations and their various consequences (see E-MINUS

Fortunate indeed is the transient who experience
many of these forms of fire, for they constitute all
that an individual needs in order to become ~~fully~~
integrated.

TREMOLO

Closely related to the phenomenon of fire is that type of reaction which is called 'tremolo'. This may appear as a violent trembling or shivering visible to the observer, or the transient may say

I have a trembly feeling in my stomach.
My eyelids seem to be twitching.
I see flickering flashes of light.
There is a trembling in such-and-such a joint.
I just feel shaky.
Every so often I feel a sudden jolt.

Sudden jolts or jerks may be quite pronounced and may affect the entire body. It is important to note that tremolo proper is not accompanied by any feeling of pain, cold, or fear; when these are present, consult the section on HISTORY. If the transient is experiencing tremolo, the observer may say

This is what we call tremolo, one of E's most useful tools. It appears to be literally a shaking free from controls and identifications, and sometimes it is very strong. It is our experience that tremolo is highly beneficial, so relax as much as you can and let your E set you free from everything that can be dislodged in this way.

Certain non-dissipative religious orders actually received their names because of the frequent appearance of tremolo among them. Thus the disciples of George Fox, an English mystic and religious revolutionary, became known as "Quakers", and the name stuck because, since they were pacifists, it also suggested 'quaking' with fear. The disciples of the American leader Mary Ann Lee became known as "Shakers". Tremolo is therefore a natural equipment of those who are close to the attainments of fire, whether this condition is arrived at as a result of E's work or as a consequence of rigid avoidance of dissipation. Many persons experience tremolo during sexual intercourse, which, at its best, is a near approach to fire.

If the tremolo seems excessively strong, the observer may say

Your E has the power to protect you from any excesses.

This is usually sufficient to reduce any superabundance of tremolo, but in very rare cases (sometimes when E's verbal communication is not well established), the tremolo may reach amazing extremes, so that the transient may say

I feel as if all the energy in the universe were flowing through my hands!   (or feet, body, etc.)

The observer may quiet such extreme activity by taking hold of the feet or hands of the transient.

POSTURING

Just as tremolo is an agitation treatment, posturing appears to be manipulation of the body by E for therapeutic purposes. There are many forms of posturing. Screwing up the eyes or shutting them very tightly or frowning — these are common forms of posturing. So are deep or rapid breathing, moving a particular limb, and changing one's position. Not infrequently the transient will seem to indulge in a vigorous self-massage, although the results of this practice are so beneficial that we suspect the real masseur of being far more skilled than any transient.

Posturing proper is not accompanied by any sensation or emotion or mental impression; when these are present, consult the section on HISTORY.

In some instances, posturing can be extremely vigorous, so much so that the first E-session in which posturing (accompanied by tremolo) was observed caused both observers present (Kitselman & Patnoude) to break out in a cold sweat, although the transient was not in the least alarmed. Posturing can also be amusing to transient as well as observer, as in the case where a grown man, who had been repressed in childhood, was impelled by his E to turn several somersaults on the bed used in the session.

38

A. L. Kitselman

HISTORY

What you are is the result of what you did with what
you were — isn't it about time you stopped? What you
will be is the result of what you do with what you are
— isn't it about time you started?

Such maxims of causal thinking are characteristic
of the view that we are the product of the past. Sometimes, however, faulty conclusions are drawn from this
point of view, such as "Our troubles exist; they are the
product of the past; therefore the past exists." This causes
a mistaken identification to appear in the mind, for
the word 'exists' refers to present time. It is more correct to say

There is no past.
There is no future.
There is only now.

Nevertheless, we do appear to contain in us a more-
or-less complete recording of all that we have experienced
in the past. Such recordings are available to us for reference purposes, but they are ordinarily mis-used
because we identify ourselves with them in some
way. For example, there is in you a recording of
what you experienced last year. If you understood
things correctly, you would realize that the person
you were last year does not exist, is dead and gone.

39

Not understanding this, you are apt to cling to last year's recording as being part of what you _are_; you _identify_ with it. In this way you give the recording power over you, you tie yourself to last year, and thus lose your ability to live and act in present time. When circumstances resembling those you recorded last year confront you in present time, you will not face them intelligently — you will do what it is recorded that you did last year. Thus, as a result of _identifying_, you operate as a mechanical recording instead of as a living, intelligent person. Some people act almost entirely from recordings; almost all of us do so at times.

E has the power to play these recordings for us and to help us dis-identify. The transient may seem _to re-experience a past incident_, and frequently this wonder is sufficient to show the transient that the incident is not real, it is only a recording, and therefore has no intelligent bearing on present time. In this way we are set free from our actions and reactions of yesterday. Some theorists maintain that this is the _only_ way in which we are set free from yesterday — that is, by experiencing the recording of an incident and dis-identifying in detail. E, however, seems to feel that this is only one of several methods.

40

E seldom plays the recording of an incident at the normal time-rate; this seems to be too slow. An incident may be presented in terms of its important factors only; this procedure is very rapid. An entire series of related incidents may be indicated in this way in just a few moments; sometimes the transient is conscious of a chain of incidents all at one time. If a transient communicates well with his E, the observer must be pretty quiet when E is handling history, for E's communication with the transient is then at a mental speed and cannot slow down to a verbal speed. In fact, Es that communicate well seldom work as slowly as verbal speed.

Certain ancient authorities say that the conscious mind is simply a consequence of the subconscious mind and the superconscious mind; it is only a by-product of the two minds of which we are not conscious. The subconscious mind seems to be a mass of identifications; several thousand years ago it was known as the 'identifier'. The superconscious mind (or E) does not seem to contain any identifications; it is said to have the power to know exactly. If this is so, the task of the conscious mind is to attempt to reconcile identifications (which are never exact) with exact knowledge (which contains no identifications), certainly a futile undertaking.

It is important for the observer to understand how the three minds are spoken to. This can be learned from Max Freedom Long: _The Secret Science Behind Miracles_. Briefly, the subconscious mind, being inferior, can be told what to do; hypnosis and most advertising methods are methods of controlling the subconscious mind. The conscious mind is rational; it can be reasoned with. Discussion and conversation are means of approaching the conscious mind. The superconscious mind or E, being superior, is never told what to do or reasoned with; it is asked to help, prayed to, invoked.

Thus the observer who attempts to direct or control E-Therapy is not in touch with E at all; only the subconscious mind responds to commands. If E is treated as an equal and approached by means of reasoning and discussion, no E is reached; only the conscious mind responds to such treatment. The observer must realize that E is very wise and knows best what to do; otherwise he is not communicating with E. The subconscious mind _obeys_; the conscious mind _reasons_; E _knows_.

The most rapid and successful E-Therapy is presided over by observers who have decided long ago that E is far smarter than they are and that the observer's job is only to assist when necessary.

Many of us were taught in school that 'things equal to the same thing are equal to each other'. In the imaginary and unreal land of pure mathematics, this is a useful rule of thought, but unfortunately our schools did not teach us that, except in the world of abstract symbols, the above quotation is a principal cause of insanity. How is this so?

In the actual, real, moving world, no two things are equal, are they? No two real things can be identical or equal. (KAPILA) As the ancient Greek Heraklides said, "You cannot step into the same river twice." (KAPILA) It may also be said that you can't speak to the same person twice. Just now, for example, the second time you read the word KAPILA you were a person who had just read the word KAPILA; the first time you read the word you were not such a person. Such differences are not necessarily trivial. If the two words 'KAPILA' had been bullets, for example, this discussion might have been much shorter.

This is no artful quibble; it is a serious statement of fact to say that your personality is a flowing, changing complex of interrelated factors. You are not the same person you were

43

a year ago. You are not the same person you were yesterday. You are not the person who started reading this. Not only that, but the person you now _are_ is the only one of you that _exists_; the person who started reading this is _gone_, _ended_, _non-existent_.

Until you understand this fully you will continue to _identify_ with persons you once were but now are not, and this will prevent you from living intelligently in present time. The persons you formerly were _do not exist_, and although you have recordings of them for reference purposes, do not make the mistake of thinking that _you_ are the recordings, for that is what we call "insanity".

Persons who live almost entirely out of recordings are seldom aware of present time reality, cannot look after themselves, and so we lock them up. Most of us live out of recordings in moments of stress and conflict; that is why we repeat ourselves so much in family quarrels, playing the same recordings over and over again for years and sometimes even decades. A very fortunate few have reached the goal E seems to intend for us; they live fully and creatively in present time and _never_ repeat recordings.

It may seem ridiculous that a rule learned in the study of mathematics could cause so much trouble in everyday living, in which so little mathematics enters. Mathematics, after all, is only a game played with symbols; why should a rule made for symbols have any influence over living realities?

Words are symbols too, you know. The two words 'KAPILA' previously quoted are equal, identical — just as $8 = 8$. Also, aqua = pani = water just as $8 = 4 + 4 = 2 + 2 + 2 + 2$. Two words can be equal in letters and/or in meaning. But no two real things are equal, so the world of words is an imaginary place like the world of numbers.

Numbers are sometimes applied to real things, but this is very dangerous. Do seven horses equal seven horses, for example? Only once in a great while, and the man who thinks otherwise should not deal in horses.

Alas! words are regularly applied to real things, and few realize the danger. Does Mary Smith resemble Mary Jones? Silly question, isn't it? Yet there are people who try to replace one Mary with another!

Nor is this verbal nonsense limited to personal problems. Why, for example, did Joseph Dzhugashvili become such a power in Russia? Partly because he adopted the name STALIN which is the Russian word for 'steel'. One of his aides uses the name MOLOTOV which means 'hammer'. Poor benighted Russians, you say. But could Theodore Underdunker become President of the United States? Or Cecil Reginald?

Your E is concerned with the words you _identify_ with. The most tricky and dangerous ones are

I me my mine myself   you your yours yourself
he or she him or her his or hers himself or herself
and your personal names.

We use these words as if they were immortal and unchanging, and they serve to _identify_ us with our recordings. In all _your_ recordings the central character is referred to as 'I' or 'me' by himself (or herself), as 'you' and 'he' or 'she', 'him' or 'her', by others. Thus these old recordings _seem_ to refer to you today, and it isn't easy for you to see that they don't. Furthermore, your recordings contain statements by other persons in which these same pronouns are used, and you may therefore have _identified_ these statements as applying to you.

46

The transients E plays recordings in order to show the transient that they are recordings, and to remove identifications. E has no other interest in recordings, and no interest in the past. E may play only snatches of recordings and the transient will appear to re-experience only bits of incidents, or E may remove identifications in other ways, without ever playing recordings. It is E who will decide to follow this course or that course, not the observer or the transient, and no session must be expected to resemble what has gone before. Observers who have been influenced by those who insist upon detailed playing of recordings as a sine quâ non of progress in integration must remember that E-Therapy is conducted by E and on the assumption that E knows what to do. It is our observation that E is interested in recordings only in certain cases, and that ten minutes of FIRE may accomplish more than many hours of HISTORY.

If a recorded incident is only partially sensed by the transient, the observer may say

Your E has the power to enable you to sense this incident in full detail, if he wishes to do so.

or Your E will show you this incident fully, if it is the wise thing to do at this time.

47

The observer must at all times remember that E is the expert in charge. Questions may be asked, if E permits. Most of the material presented in these pages was learned from watching E s at work and asking them questions. Just as a young interne might assist a great surgeon at the operating table, so must the observer assist the transient's E. Both interne and observer are eager to learn, anxious to keep out of the way, and ready to help in any indicated way. Either might ask an occasional question, but neither would ever dream of telling the great expert what to do.

As an observer gains experience, he will develop faith and confidence in the incredible efficiency of E and in the efficacy of E-Therapy. This confidence will keep him from talking too much, and he will realize that no E-observer with reasonable good sense will be more effective than any other E-observer with reasonable good sense, for it is the transient's E who does the therapy. This is literally true in all typical E-cases, in which E communicates well with the transient, and sixty to eighty percent of all persons are typical E-cases. Thus there is no occasion for snobbery among E-observers.

STRATEGY

When it is impractical or inconvenient to remove an identification directly, E has recourse to strategy. In general, E-strategy is as follows:

The transient finds himself in a situation which E has constructed — that is, the transient has the experience of being somewhere, and this 'somewhere' is <u>not</u> a recording; it is a scene <u>produced</u> <u>by</u> E.

In this situation, E indicates that the transient is to perform some act — such as open a door, cross a bridge, climb a tree, throw a ball, etc.

For some reason, the transient finds this difficult to do, and says so.

Being coaxed and urged on by the observer, the transient succeeds in doing what E has requested.

These four elements —— a situation, an indicated action, reluctance, and final accomplishment —— constitute typical E-strategy. Although the situation which E produces is 'imaginary', it is not consciously 'imagined' by the transient, nor does he find it too easy to do what E indicates. Let us examine the notes of the first E-strategy case:

Date: September 3, 1950
Observer: A. L. Kitselman, who has observed five transients for a total of six hours of E-Therapy.
Transient: Preston A. Patnoude, who has been 'audited' for thirty hours of 'dianetic processing', a procedure designed by L. R. Hubbard to evoke the eighth power of E and control it at will. Although Hubbard's method is often successful, it has failed completely with this transient. Patnoude, however, was the first observer of _fire_ in E-Therapy (see page 5) on August 29, and witnessed the first appearance of _tremolo_ and ~~posturing~~ on September 1 (transient: Mrs. Nora King — observer: A. L. Kitselman).

I just saw a door slam shut, very hard. It is sprung and wedged in place — it slammed so hard. · · · · · This seems to be the control circuits which keep me from recalling incidents. · · · · As I was saying that, the door was barricaded with strips of wood nailed across it.
~~Look around.~~ Perhaps you can find a hammer — a claw hammer, maybe.
There's a sledge hammer over here to one side.
Use it to batter through the door.

50

No, that doesn't work; I'm on the wrong side of the door. I only wedged the door in tighter.

Look around for a crowbar or something.

Yes, here's a crowbar — a nice heavy one.

See if you can pry the door open.

All right · · · · · (several minutes elapse) · · · ·

How are things now?

I can see through the bottom corner now.

Can you get through the opening?

No, it's too small.

Well, do what you can to get the whole door open.

All right. · · · · (several more minutes) · · · · The door just fell through and disappeared.

What do you see through the door?

Just blackness — I can't see anything.

Go stand in the door and look through. What do you see now?

Nothing — just blackness.

See if there is a light switch.

Yes, I found one over here on the side.

Well, turn it on.

I did, but it didn't work.

Very well. Walk straight ahead now, and watch for a light.

51

All right. · I've moved forward one step, and I don't see anything yet.
Take another step.
I have.
Don't hesitate; go right ahead. If, as you say, the closed door represented the control circuits which obstructed your ability to recall incidents, I think they are all cleared away now, and you can recall events without difficulty.
· · · · · I just tested what you said, and you are right; I <u>can</u> recall incidents now. I'm walking ahead now.
What do you see?
I see a clip-board lying there ahead of me with a bunch of papers on it.
Go forward and pick it up — see what's on the papers.
They are notes of some kind — probably the things that have happened to me.
Look closely — what do they say?
It's all faded away now — my E seems to be through for the day.
How do you feel?
Fine.
(elapsed time : 30 minutes)

52

This first strategy case is more or less typical. The door which the transient saw was the first thing he had ever seen clearly and lastingly with his eyes closed. His struggle to pry open the door was very real to him, for although no external motion was visible to the observer, the transient's replies to questions were spoken as if he were perspiring and short of breath. Also, what E accomplished was also very real, for the transient could recall incidents after this session.

E frequently represents the whole catalogue of recorded incidents as a kind of 'hall of time', as in this case. This 'hall of time' may appear as a long tunnel or pipe or scenic railway or road; the observer's task is usually to coax the transient to enter and travel as far as possible.

Or, E's strategy may consist entirely of an 'obstacle course' of one situation after another, some of them quite childish. One transient, who had been dominated by an older sister when a child, was directed to 'murder' her in various ways in a number of strategy situations. Again, E may simply show a pleasant scene at the end of a session to indicate that all is well.

Strategy is simply a name for any and all special tactics employed by E, and it may take many forms. It is strategy, for example, to put the observer into turn-off so that he will not become restless and interfere with the transient's turn-off, as E frequently does. Special information is sometimes given to the observer by E, as will be shown in the E-plus section.

The observer must remember that E will decide whether or not the transient is to understand any special symbolism in a strategy situation. When in doubt, ask E what to do. If E presents a strategy situation but does not communicate well enough to say what is to be done, the observer must suggest whatever seems most likely.

Strategy is most successful when the transient uses all available strength of will and force of imagination in doing as E directs. E seems to use the will-power the transient produces in order to effect the forceful removal of deep-seated identifications which the transient cannot conveniently or comfortably face directly. Thus the indirect method of E's strategy is a very valuable and powerful aid in the work of personal integration.

54

ARGUMENT

It is not necessary for a transient to _believe_ in E-Therapy in order to experience results; in fact, very few persons have any appreciation of the reality of E until they have experienced results themselves or observed them in a number of cases. Nevertheless, strong beliefs can block the work of E, and it is necessary to take steps to put such beliefs to one side during sessions. Any belief or opinion which questions the operation of E-Therapy may interfere with the work of E. Suppose that a session begins with ten minutes of normal consciousness and then the transient says

I wish my E would start to work, or
Why doesn't something happen? or
I sure hope I have an E.

These statements are the equivalent of saying

My E isn't working. It doesn't work. or
Unless something happens, I'm out of luck. or
I'd like to have an E, but I haven't got one.

The observer must counter such remarks with

Are you _sure_ your E isn't working now? or
Something _may_ be happening _now_. or
Isn't that like hoping you have a brain?

55

It is not the observer's task to refute or defeat the objections of the transient; all that is needed is to induce the transient to suspend the objections until after the session. If the transient says

This whole idea of a super-smart mind in me that I've never known about is perfectly ridiculous!

A tactful observer will reply

Yes, it does seem rather preposterous, I know. But we'll never really know whether or not it is ridiculous unless we test it with an open mind, will we?

This sort of thing is called 'argument' because in the transient's mind there is an argument with E-Therapy which the observer must suspend until the transient's E can present his case; it is not an argument between transient and observer. All E asks is a trial; after the trial the transient may be the judge and render an opinion. It is simply not good practice to render a decision before a trial or without a trial.

A certain amount of argument takes place in the transient's mind long before any sessions take place; the questions on page 8 are typical. The transient's views are to be modified by the observer only in so far as they impede the work of E; otherwise they are not to be challenged.

56

The original writing on E-Therapy was mimeo-graphed in September of 1950 in Honolulu. It was based upon some sixty E-sessions in which some twenty-odd transients were observed by Kitselman and Patnoude. At this time E-Therapy was outlined as follows:

STARTING WORK

ASKING
TURN-OFF

EASY WORK

FIRE
TREMOLO
POSTURING
HISTORY

DIFFICULT WORK

STRATEGY
ARGUMENT

As these words were written E-Therapy was in its second year, and no alteration in the above structural outline had become necessary as yet. Familiarity with these three stages and eight factors is familiarity with E-Therapy.

In this outline, <u>strategy</u> and <u>argument</u> are labeled <u>difficult</u> <u>work</u> because they call for active participation on the part of the observer, participation in which skill and understanding are important factors. This skill and understanding may be acquired through patient observing of E at work and through the study of E-minus material. The following examples of argument and how to cope with it may be of assistance:

(Note: Use no more of the argument-countering material than is needed; the full treatment here given is required only in extreme cases. The observer's job is only to counter, not to instruct; E will instruct.)

Shouldn't I keep reporting everything to you? Why should you? Might that not get in E's way? Why should I know any more than enough to tell me how things are going? Am I giving you this therapy, or is E? Shouldn't you be primarily concerned with your E, rather than with me? If you occupy yourself with talking to me, are you relaxing and letting E work? After all, your E is in charge here: if he wants you to report to me, do so; if not, just watch what he does.

58

I don't like this business of referring to E as a separate, independent mind.

Have we said, 'separate'? Where did you get the idea that your E is separate from you? Don't you see that if you think of your E as a separate entity, and then deny the existence of such an entity, your mind will reject automatically anything that E tries to do for you? If you seize upon reasons to reject E, are you giving him a fair trial?

We do say that E is more-or-less independent, but this is our observation, rather than a fixed theory. Many transients have found that they can experience turn-off or fire, for example, when they ask E for it, but not when they try to achieve these experiences without asking E. A few are able to experience turn-off or fire at will. Thus E appears to act independently in the majority of cases.

As you become better acquainted with your E, you can test these matters yourself and draw your own conclusions. In the meantime, suppose we suspend judgment until we can find out what your E can do for you. Let's throw all objections overboard and let E go to work.

In that section on __asking__ you attempt to explain away a lot of objections to E-Therapy by comparing E with a wise man. This visualizing of E as a wise man seems ridiculous to me.

Then don't visualize E as a wise man. The point is that there is a part of your mind which is free from motivations and which doesn't become active unless you furnish a motivation by consciously or unconsciously asking for help. This is not the easiest thing in the world to understand, and the personal illustration of a wise man living next door serves to convey this information. Everything in the section you mention can be understood in a de-personalized way if you prefer it. After all, a wise man may be assumed to be someone with a strong and active E, and the behavior of a wise man as a person must resemble the behavior of E as a part of the mind.

We do not know the nature of E. If there is something in us which opposes the work of E, this opposition is apt to take the form of convictions that E is personal or impersonal, organic or inorganic, physical or mental, etc., and rejection of E-Therapy on the basis of these convictions. Let's put such quibbling aside.

I object to this personifying of E as the examiner, monitor, integrator, etc., and the use of personal pronouns when referring to E.

Then refer to E as the examining, monitoring, integrating, etc., process or activity or function, and use the pronoun 'it'. Or, if you wish to avoid both extremes, use the term 'E' as both noun and pronoun.

E is an <u>aspect</u> of a human being, a person, a man or a woman or a child. It has been indicated by several advanced E-transients that "E is what we are when there is turn-off" and that "turn-off is suspension of the identifying process". If this is so, it may be proper to refer to E in the same way that we refer to a human being, a person, a man or a woman or a child.

Again, E is observed to be an intelligence of extremely high order. If you think that such a high intelligence must necessarily be mechanical, inorganic, or abstract, then refer to E as 'it'. If you think that such a high intelligence must necessarily be human, personal, or organic, refer to E as 'him' or 'her'.

You are at liberty to refer to E in the way that suits you best.

I want to achieve such-and-such. (supernormal recall, clairvoyance, healing power, artistic talent, increased earning capacity, release from some trouble, position, reputation, skill, etc.)

~~Doesn't~~ this amount to telling E what to do? If you tell E what to do, you aren't talking to your E — although you may indeed be talking to some part of your mind which will get you what you want. There are many forms of faith healing and so-called 'mental science' which will sometimes get you what you want. Which is more important, to get what you want, or to achieve permanent personal integration? Asserting or affirming or imagining something may help you get what you want; but it will not help you become integrated. Getting what you want without becoming integrated is far worse than becoming integrated without getting what you want. Becoming integrated, however, will solve all your problems, either by getting what you want or by getting rid of the want.

Let us concern ourselves, then, with asking E for help — without specifying. If what we want is wise, E will give it; if not, E will cure us of wanting it. First let us become integrated, and all other things will be taken care of.

62

I have decided that E is such-and-such. (the astral body, the matrix of intentions, the atman, the unconscious, the guardian angel), a deva, etc.)

Perhaps you are right. However, it will be better for you to temporarily suppress this conviction of yours, because we have found that a fixed conception of what E is (even though it may be true) is likely to hinder E from working freely.

You see, your conception of E is a product of your mind, and, until you become fully integrated, a part of your mind consists of false information. Your conception of E may be partially based upon false information, no matter how clear it may seem to you now. Such a conception is perfectly acceptable as a temporary opinion of what E is, but it will obstruct your personal integration if you see it as a certainty.

After all, it is more important for you to let your E give you therapy than it is for you to make theories about E. In general, it seems that transients progress more rapidly when they do not theorize about the nature of E. Theories usually are used in place of realities. Your E is here now; you need no theory about it.

63

It seems to me that the claims made on behalf of E-Therapy are preposterous — the results to be expected, for example, and the ten powers.

Accept only what you wish to accept. The list of results to be expected is intended primarily to answer the question, "What is E-Therapy for?". The items listed are widely known consequences of personal integration and many of them have appeared during and after E-Therapy. Certainly the widely known consequences of personal integration in general may be expected by those who take up E-Therapy in particular.

As for the ten powers of E, they have all been observed in prodigies of various sorts and in E-transients in varying degrees of effectiveness. If you doubt the existence of extra-sensory perception in general, it may help you to read 'The Reach of the Mind' by J. B. Rhine. On the other hand, if you have a deep and abiding belief in the rightness of orthodox science, you should carefully read 'The Books of Charles Fort' (published by Holt). You don't have to accept anything in order to progress in E-Therapy, but you should suspend your objections temporarily — at least during the period of therapy.

I doubt that I have an E.

Do you doubt that you have a mind?

Yes, I doubt that, too.

Why?

Because I have been studying the modern 'operational' school of psychology.

Is this the school which doubts the existence of all things which cannot be observed externally?

Yes. Terms such as 'feeling', 'mind', 'wisdom', 'happiness', etc., are all considered suspect.

How about the term 'itch'?

Unless a man is observed to scratch himself, we cannot say that he itches.

Have you ever itched without scratching?

Yes.

Is an itch that isn't scratched less real than an itch that is scratched?

No — an itch that isn't scratched is usually more real than one that is scratched.

But doesn't the 'operational' school tend toward the opposite view?

Yes.

Then, are the views of this school realistic? Aren't they false information, and don't they obstruct personal integration rather than produce it?

I strongly believe in psychic phenomena and I am guided by discarnate entities, by spirits.

Can spirits communicate directly with everyone?

No. Few entities are strong enough to communicate with anyone who is not psychically sensitive.

Does one entity ever impersonate another?

Yes, sometimes this will be done — either as a joke or for some serious purpose.

Then let me point out something to you. E is an entity which can communicate with sixty to eighty percent of the population; this means that E is at least a hundred times more powerful than any other communicating entity. Also, we know that in E-strategy, E can create situations which the transient cannot tell from the real thing, and in these situations E frequently impersonates many persons. E can also produce extraordinary phenomena of many kinds such as turn-off, fire, tremolo, etc. Now the question is — since E is so powerful and so wise and so able, <u>how</u> do we <u>know</u> <u>that</u> all <u>psychic</u> <u>phenomena</u> <u>are</u> <u>not</u> <u>produced</u> by <u>E</u>? In short, if the spirit of your uncle George communicates with you, is it really uncle George, or is it your E impersonating your uncle George in order to help you? Can you answer this question?

I think that it is preposterous to speak of recalling early events such as birth or events before birth, and this business of 'former lives' is fantastic and absurd.

Why?

Because of what we know about the structure and growth of the nervous system.

Aren't you assuming that the recalling of events requires a nervous system?

Why, certainly.

Well, of course, you may be right. It may be that all such apparent recalls are constructed by E for therapeutic purposes, and have no basis in fact. Who can say? On the other hand, the existence of extra-sensory faculties has been accepted by all scientific authorities competent to pass upon the evidence — and this ever since 1938. (See 'The Reach of the Mind' by Dr. J. B. Rhine.) Little or nothing is known among scientists about the structural nature of the extra-sensory faculties, and this same vagueness may characterize scientific knowledge about the structural basis of recall. We know far too little about structure, at least in scientific circles, to be able to say with certainty that something is preposterous or absurd.

I am a religious man, and it seems to me that asking for the help of E is the same thing as praying to God. Why shouldn't I just pray to God for what I want?

So far as we know, it is quite accurate to refer to E as the father within, the holy spirit, the comforter, the witness, or the messiah. If you regard God as an intelligent transforming power within you, praying to God is equivalent to asking E. But if the God to whom you pray is a static picture of belief, you are hampering your E with fixed ideas. Most religious people pray to a God who is remote from them, an abstract product of tradition and belief, and such an inanimate deity is not very effective. A fortunate few, however, pray to a God who is a live wire within, and to such as these the Lord's Prayer is an asking of E.

Another point: praying to God for what you want is telling God what to do, and this is against the rules. If you want God's help, ask for it, but let God decide what form it will take — unless you think you are wiser than God.

If God is thought of as having the ten powers, then E-Therapy is God-Therapy. Will you try it?

I say That you have made extravagant claims That are misleading, and worse, because they will turn the best minds against E-Therapy as a crackpot proposition. The claims may be true, but you will have a difficult time proving it.

In E-Therapy it is E who does the proving; we observers make no efforts to persuade. If you are interested in E-Therapy, we will help you, but we have no desire to convert anyone. You must decide for yourself what your attitude will be.

We are inclined to feel that the people who are interested in E-Therapy are motivated by their own Es and do not need to be persuaded. We work for E and for the people E brings us, and those who prefer to live without E-Therapy may have very good reasons for it.

We assume that the 'best minds' you speak of are members of the academic and professional fields who generally prefer a conservative and dignified approach. Such 'best minds' have usually been the last to recognize any true innovation, and we are making no effort to seek their approval. We try to avoid the academic extreme of skepticism and the religious extreme of credulity in telling the truth about E-Therapy as we see it.

I am very happily married, and I am afraid that E-Therapy may make me less responsive to my husband. I don't want to become too detached.

There isn't anything negative about personal integration; you will never become more integrated than you want to be.

The sexual relationship involves turn-off of the world's irritations, and one's quality of response varies accordingly. The best sexual response is fire, and well-integrated persons regard sex as a means to fire. The next best response is tremolo, which is often accompanied by some fire. The next best response is delight in the body and in its sexual posturing. Some people find pleasure in the sexual relationship because of the circumstances surrounding it (romance, intrigue, adventure, etc.); they enjoy its place in history. Others respond when sex is successful strategy, a means to an end, and still others enter into the sexual relationship vindictively, as a form of combat or argument.

E-Therapy will help you climb this ladder of responses until you are completely fulfilled in them. Your E will show you what is beyond sex when you are ready, but not before.

70

I am about to marry a very beautiful woman who is much admired by other men. What I want from E-Therapy is the power to keep her happy with me.

You will get the power you want much more quickly if you do not specifically ask for it. A beautiful woman who has many admirers is most attracted (if she is in good health) to a man who is physically, emotionally, and mentally integrated, and of these three qualities the most important is mental integration or insight. The man who has acquired insight sees deeply into people and relationships, and intrigues the lady of beauty because he is not carried away by her power to attract. Such a man is a master of beauty rather than mastered by it. The man who has accumulated understanding is described in "Song of the Answerer" by Walt Whitman, and his power over beauty is described in "the Fountainhead" by Ayn Rand.

If you give yourself into the hands of your E, and make a special study of E-minus material, you will become the kind of man who need never fear competition, and your wife will achieve the happiness which so few beautiful women know how to find.

71

I don't see how E-Therapy can help me because it is a rigid technique, and I do not think any crystallized technique can benefit the mind.

You apparently are assuming that the three stages and eight factors constitute a technique. They do not; they are simply a catalogue of things E has been observed to do, and could probably be presented in eight stages and seventy-three factors. There is nothing rigid in this catalogue of effects. The only technique in E-Therapy is to let E decide what technique to use, and E seems to know them all and use a good many. E-Therapy consists in calling in a _therapist_ _who_ _knows_ _exactly_ _what_ _to_ _do_ — and leaving all choice of method or technique up to him.

These examples of argument and its countering will help the observer to understand the art, and experience in watching Es at work will complete his education. All of this material that is helpful has been learned from various Es; the part that isn't helpful is the contribution of the writer's identifications. Whoever can successfully subtract the latter from the former will master the art of E-observing.

72

E-PLUS

If the transient's E does not appear to be very effective, the observer may ask

Does E wish me to assist actively?

In an E-Therapy case the answer will be negative, and the observer may practice the virtue of patience. But if the answer is "yes", or if there is no answer, 'E-plus' is required. 'E-plus therapy is 'E plus active assistance' therapy. In this therapy the relation between the transient's E and the observer is like that existing between the director and the assistant director in a motion picture company. Just as the motion picture director makes all vital decisions, while the assistant director does most of the work of managing the company, so in E-plus therapy the transient's E indicates and directs what is to be done, leaving the observer the task of conducting the actual operations. E-plus therapy is therapy in which the observer acts as an assistant E, using his own best judgment and doing what he has seen Es do.

Thus only experienced E-observers are qualified to do E-plus therapy, and the subject cannot be discussed in detail in such a work as this. Before

73

very long a serviceable E-plus text, containing the findings of many experienced observers, will be available. Nevertheless, certain useful stratagems may be presented here.

If E has asked for active assistance, the observer may say

Will E please give me a clue to work on?

E usually answers this request by showing the transient some scene or incident, and the task of the observer is to help the transient obtain a closer understanding of the scene or incident shown. This may be done by asking questions or having the transient repeat some phrase related to the incident, or in one of several other ways. In some cases, the observer may ask

What is obstructing the work of E?

E may then indicate in some way what the observer and transient should do in order to make suitable contact with E, and the case then becomes a regular E-case.

One experienced observer (Adams) reports that many transients prevent themselves from entering into therapy by trying too hard to get phenomena and having too strong an attitude of expectancy. This tenseness and rigidity of attitude can indeed be a serious obstacle. In such cases, the observer may say

Suppose nothing happens in this session — not even any turn-off. Let's even suppose that nothing happens in the next five or six sessions. Will the world come to an end? Won't you go on living just about as usual, just as you have been doing?

This tactic is sufficient in most cases to cause the transient to discard the fixed attitude as ridiculous, and E can proceed with therapy.

Alcoholics and other persons who may not be able to give their attention properly may be helped by the methods set forth in _Client-Centered Therapy_ by Dr. Carl Rogers; these methods are verbal counseling techniques which may be applied in ordinary conversation. Dr. Rogers' book is recommended as an authoritative text on many of the factors involved in E-Therapy, a thoroughgoing and worth-while book.

Another important E-plus procedure is for the observer to try to 'coach' the transient into turn-off, pointing out that one shouldn't try to _make_ the mind quiet — just let it wander, watching it without approving or disapproving — and it will gradually become quiet. This method is frequently successful.

There is an interesting form of E-plus therapy which may be called 'E-double-plus' or 'hyper-E'. This consists in having the observer's E tell the observer what to do to help the transient achieve contact with his own E.

Sounds miraculous, doesn't it?

Some observers found that they could tell, <u>without</u> <u>looking</u>, when a transient was in turn-off. They didn't know how they knew, but they were always right. Apparently their Es told them.

Some transients can tell whether or not a number is prime (a prime number is one such as 2, 3, 5, 7, ... 127, 4481 which is <u>not</u> divisible by any other prime number) <u>instantly</u> and <u>without</u> <u>calculating</u>. Apparently their Es tell them.

All these prodigies are powers of E.

Now let a transient who cannot contact his E work with an observer who has good contact with <u>his</u> E. Can't the transient's E communicate directly with the observer's E? Can't the observer's E tell the observer what to do, or what to tell the transient? Doesn't this amount to indirect contact between the transient and his own E?

That is hyper-E. The difficulty is that observers who have such good contact are not yet very numerous.

76

A still rarer form of E-plus therapy may be called 'E-triple-plus' or 'fire transmission'. This consists in transmitting fire into a transient who needs it in order to contact his E, for it has been found that persons who have fire in abundance can transmit it to others who lack it. The transients E can work with the fire thus received, and much can be accomplished in a short time. Again, persons who have fire in abundance are still comparatively rare.

Nevertheless, there is a natural balance in these matters. The general population can be divided into four classes:

1. those who can respond to E-Therapy.
2. those who need E+ or assisted-E-Therapy.
3. those who need E++ or hyper-E-Therapy.
4. those who need E+++ or fire-transmission therapy.

Now it so happens that E-Therapy is not difficult to learn; enough people can become E-observers to help all those who can respond to E-Therapy. Of these E-observers, a sufficient number can provide E+ for all who need it, a smaller number can provide hyper-E for the smaller number who need it, and a few can provide sufficient fire transmission for the few who need it.

77

What of the recalcitrant husband or wife or parent or child who is hostile to the idea of therapy? A surprisingly large percentage of the people seem to feel that they are all right as they are and need no improvement, and some of these are so full of tension that they irritate others. How can one help a child who is too young to understand the idea of a 'magic friend' inside? How can E-therapy be given to a deaf person, or to a person who is otherwise prevented from entering into a session?

Es have told us how. Let A observe B in an E-session, both asking their Es (and C's E) to let C's tensions and identifications be released _through_ B. B thus acts as a _proxy_ for C. This can be done without C's knowledge, for when C's tensions are sufficiently released, C's E may impel C to express an interest in receiving therapy.

Incredible? Ask those who have tried it.

It is also possible to do this without an observer; B can ask that C's tensions be transferred to C and there released.

Of course, E-Therapy _is_ impossible (to some), and hyper-E is miraculous. Yet there comes a time when observers can say, "The _impossible_ we _do_ _immediately;_ the _miraculous_ _takes_ a _little_ _longer._"

E-MINUS

The words 'I am' are potent words;
be careful what you hitch them to.
The thing you're claiming has a way
of reaching back and claiming you!

The removal of identifications is the entire task of E. It is a subject that E knows all about. Nevertheless, the conscious mind can learn much about dis-identifying, and this is a great help. E-minus is the art of conscious dis-identifying, and it is called 'E-minus' because it does not depend upon E at all and can be done by persons in whom E does not manifest.

A certain amount of E-minus information is useful to anyone; Es teach a great deal of it. Pages 43, 44, 45 & 46 contain E-minus information; go back and look at them now.

―――――

Each thing, person, or idea is changeable, uncertain, subject to change without notice; even though some ideas may seem to be permanent, we who think of them do so in changing ways. This is something nobody denies. Yet we habitually identify these changeable, unpredictable factors of life with words and symbols which do not change.

This causes a great deal of mischief. It causes us to expect things, people, and ideas to be more stable and reliable than they are capable of being in this changeable world; such expectations are a major cause of conflict and suffering.

Suppose that two variables called 'John' and 'Mary' get 'married'. For a year they complement one other, living together in 'pleasant harmony'. Then 'John' flows into a phase called 'alcoholism' and 'Mary' is transformed into 'frigidity'; the relationship called 'pleasant harmony' has ceased to exist. The two variables manifest 'bitterness' and 'resentment'.

Why? 'Pleasant harmony' is guaranteed to no one, yet 'John' and 'Mary' feel that they have been 'betrayed' and 'defrauded'.

The trouble here is that two variables thought they were constants, misled by the constants 'John' and 'Mary', for the names were constant.

Had the two variables fully realized that they were variables, the phases called 'alcoholism' and 'frigidity' might have appeared, but there would have been less 'bitterness' and 'resentment', and this in turn would have resulted in less 'alcoholism' and 'frigidity'.

Misinformation about variableness is a deadly thing.

Now how can knowledge of this kind help you?

Well, first of all, you see that it is so. You see the suffering that appears in people because they mistakenly thought a variable was a constant.

Secondly, you understand how it works. The entire mechanism of conflict begins to reveal itself to you.

Thirdly, you become better integrated, for conflicts which you understand no longer arise in you.

Fourthly, your mind is improved. As a result of your integration, your faculties are now clear and sharp.

Fifthly, you fully understand, for your insight is now so penetrating that you can help others as well as yourself.

Sixthly, you become fully integrated, and are permanently freed from all forms of suffering caused by misinformation about variableness. All the other advantages of full integration are yours to enjoy and to use in helping others achieve their integration.

Now, this is not a text in E-minus subject matter; our purpose is only to show what E-minus is. Fortunately, there are some good books available which contain much valuable material, and it is recommended that you make use of them. Certainly there is no field of investigation which will better equip you to be an observer.

81

Which are the books which contain E-minus information? Some are fiction and some are non-fiction. If you like Emerson's essays, read and study them. One of the best American sources of E-minus thinking is the book 'Leaves of Grass' by Walt Whitman, also his 'Preface to the 1855 Edition'. A later E-minus writer, especially helpful to persons who take scientific orthodoxy too seriously, was Charles Fort (see 'The Books of Charles Fort', published by Holt). A powerful novel with some E-minus teaching is 'The Fountainhead' by Ayn Rand, and similar messages are to be found in 'Jean-Christophe' by Romain Rolland, and 'The Moon and Sixpence' by Somerset Maugham. Aldous Huxley's 'After Many a Summer Dies the Swan' contains interesting observations, as does 'Hypatia' by Charles Kingsley. Difficult reading, but interesting to some, are 'All and Everything' by G. Gurdjieff and 'Science and Sanity' by A. Korzybski.

Socrates was an E-minus therapist, and his more characteristic dialogues are worth consulting, as well as his 'Apology'. Reading 'Flatland' by Edwin Abbott will exercise the E-minus muscles, as will 'The Philosophy of As If' by Vaihinger. Those who like science-fiction will find E-minus thinking in the novels of E.E. Smith and the 'A' novels of A. E. Van Vogt.

Devotees of the exotic in literature will find E-minus material in 'A Dweller on Two Planets' by 'Phylos', and in 'The Ninth Vibration', 'The Key of Dreams', 'The Perfume of the Rainbow', 'The Treasure of Ho' and other books by L. Adams Beck. Adventure stories with an E-minus background are 'Tros of Samothrace', 'Black Light', and 'The Devil's Guard' by Talbot Mundy, and 'The Fuse' and 'The World Emperor' by P.B.A.

'A Search in Secret India' by Paul Brunton contains interviews with some E-minus thinkers, as does 'God is my Adventure' by Rom Landau. 'Philosophies of India by Zimmer is a good general text, but the best detailed treatment of the Oriental E-minus teachings is 'The Time Teachers' by P.B.A.

An outstanding teacher of E-minus integration, an Oriental by birth but an Occidental in upbringing, is living at the time of this writing. This man, Jiddu Krishnamurti (1895→), has reached the goal that E intends for us (if _this_ writer is any judge), and his extemporaneous talks are very useful to those who can understand them. A publication list can be had from Krishnamurti Writings, Inc., Ojai, California, or, if you are in a hurry, send twenty dollars and ask for 'all the talks'. We know several who have done this, and none of them regret it.

It has been said that there are three kinds of teachers — worldly, unworldly, and integrative. The worldly teachers are those who accept man as he is in his normal worldly state, and endeavour to work out laws and principles which make or-derly living possible — teachers such as Hammurabi, Manu, Moses, Confucius, Machiavelli, Blackstone, Marx, Freud and Emily Post. The unworldly teachers are opposed to the worldly life and seek to interest us in the 'higher' life, favoring fire as opposed to sex, monasticism as opposed to the married state, asceticism as opposed to the pursuit of pleasure and gain, idealism as opposed to ag-nosticism, mentalism as opposed to materialism, faith as opposed to skepticism, etc. —— teachers such as the great mystics and occultists, Mother Ann Lee, George Fox, Sri Ramakrishna, Sri Chaitanya, Manly Hall and many ministers. The integrative teachers do not take sides in this con-flict between the worldly and unworldly elements; they are concerned with the integrative transformation of the individual into a condition that is more spon-taneous and less mechanical, more free and less bound —teachers such as Socrates, Whitman, Emerson, Kapila, Krishna, Lao Tzu ··· anyone like your E.

84

Now there are four degrees of integration which are attainable by E-minus methods, with or without the help of E. The first degree of integration is achieved when one fully understands what full integration is and how to attain it. Such a person _sees_ the goal and how to reach it, and thereby becomes free from all beliefs, speculations, and opinions about the nature of personal integration. Being free from theories, this person is _theoretically free_ and has the assurance of arriving eventually at _practical freedom_ or full integration, for the attainment is permanent and irreversible; the total amputation of speculative beliefs is no less permanent than any other amputation. This condition of _assurance_ is achieved by an act of understanding or insight or comprehension; there is no work to do other than this.

If the assured person takes up the work of dis-identifying, a second degree of freedom or integration is reached; this involves an emotional integration and lessening of dissipative factors to such an extent that some fire is experienced.

If a twice-freed person proceeds to eliminate all forms of physical dissipation so that fire-experiences may be attained, the third freedom is reached, a condition devoid of physical identifications.

Finally, if a thrice-freed person proceeds to remove all identifications without remainder and become one who is spontaneous and free from the re-playing of recordings, the condition achieved is full integration. Such a person never again suffers fear, hatred, or grief.

On page 30 four drives are mentioned — those toward

physical fulfilment   (personal),
emotional fulfilment   (relational),
mental fulfilment   (associational), and
ultimate fulfilment   (transcendental).

The fourth of these drives, which causes us to seek out a religion or a philosophy, an answer to ultimate questions, is permanently satisfied by the first freedom.

The third of these drives, which causes us to seek out mental companionship in organizations, groups, societies, is permanently satisfied by the second freedom.

The second of these drives, which causes us to seek out emotional companions, lovers, family relationships, stimulants and entertainments, is permanently satisfied by the third freedom.

The first of these drives, which causes us to be preoccupied with our own happiness, our own security, and with having our own way, is permanently satisfied by the fourth freedom.

It is possible for you to become fully integrated.

QUALIFICATIONS

Are you a good transient? Are you a good observer? Is E-Therapy a good therapy? Is the writer of these pages qualified to present it? Has he done a good job?

These are important questions and must be considered carefully.

What must you do to be a good transient?

1. Recognize that your E is not interested in converting you to any fixed 'ism' or belief. If you feel inclined to identify yourself with any exclusive ideology, that is an identification — it is not the intention of your E.

2. Recognize that your E never compels you to do anything; E has no wish to dominate. If you think you are 'commanded' to recite a prayer on a street-corner or commit adultery with a neighbor, that is not your E; E does not command

3. Recognize that your E does not insist upon a fixed nomenclature or vocabulary, you are at liberty to call E-Therapy itself and the phenomena observed in it by any names you please. If you do not like this writer's method of presenting E-Therapy, use or write your own presentation.

4. Recognize that the process of becoming integrated involves changing; be prepared to change. Your past conditioning shows in your indulgences and irritations; make an effort to avoid both. If one of your indulgences is smoking, for example, cut down on it until you aren't getting much pleasure out of it, but not so much that you are irritated by having so few smokes. This puts you in neutral gear, so to speak, so that transformation is possible. And don't take a free ride in E-Therapy; if you aren't exchanging sessions with someone, pay your observer enough for his time so that you are not exploiting him, but not so much that he is exploiting you. In all these matters, let your motto be, " neither too much nor too little ".

5. Don't try to dominate your E or your observer, and don't expect either of them to dominate you. Be neither authoritative nor subservient. Look upon your E as your companion, guide and friend — and look upon your observer as the friend with whom you visit E.

6. Don't expect your E and your observer to do all the work of integrating you. Observe yourself, your thoughts, words, and actions — without approval or disapproval — constantly, as E does.

What must you do to be a good observer?

1. Never let your pet ideologies intrude into your E-work. No matter how enthusiastic a Rosicrucian, Theosophist, semanticist, sociologist, physical culturist, spiritualist, yogi or commissar you may be, keep it to yourself when in contact with transients. If your conversation before, during and after sessions is full of your opinions and interpretations from (for example) the point of view of a psychic, you are not competent to act as an E-observer. Fully competent E, E+, E++, and E+++ observers should have attained the first, second, third and fourth degrees of integration (see pages 85 & 86); you should try for the first, at least.

2. In E-Therapy, don't tell E or the transient what to do, and in the E-plus therapies do as little of this as possible.

3. Don't stick to a fixed vocabulary, you and your transients will get tired of any standard nomenclature. It doesn't matter in the least what you <u>call</u> what you do, it is the <u>doing</u> that is important.

4. Don't exploit others, and don't let yourself be exploited. Either exchange your services as an observer for other services, or charge for them — neither too much nor too little.

5. Don't become an ardent admirer of your own intelligence; don't become an ardent admirer of someone else's intelligence. Don't be a leader or a follower, and avoid those persons who expect you to be either.

6. Watch yourself in your work as an observer — look at your motivations and be mindful of them.

    Is E-Therapy a good therapy?

1. It has no fixed or exclusive theory or system.

2. It is not a therapy in which one person controls another; the observer does not endanger the transient.

3. No fixed vocabulary or nomenclature is required.

4. It is not an exploitive therapy.

5. It does not proceed from some arbitrary center of authority and orthodoxy; no subservience is required.

6. It is spreading and growing on its merits alone; no salesmanship or propaganda is involved.

    Is the writer of these pages qualified to present it?

1. He has achieved the first degree of integration by E-methods (1936), but has not yet responded well as an E-transient (there is some response to E+, E++, and E+++). Thus he is slow in integration.

2. He intends these pages as a letter of introduction; they are not an authoritative text.

3. He recommends the use of a flexible nomenclature.

4. He is anxious neither to exploit nor be exploited.

5. He will accept co-conspirators but not disciples, and expects the same courtesy from others.

6. Having accomplished the task of writing these pages, he refuses to be identified with E-Therapy as a movement and is going on to other things.

Thus this writer is apparently competent enough to prepare this 'letter of introduction', but neither experienced enough nor otherwise qualified to speak on the subject in any authoritative way. In good time we may expect more thoroughgoing material from other persons more painstaking.

Nevertheless, even this short 'letter of introduction' contains serious omissions:

Herbert A. Werthauer, in the early days of E-work, observed (it may well be called Werthauer's principle) "let E decide when the session is to end — that is, let E end the session when E wishes to do so — and the transient will always feel at least as well as when the session started".

Henry Hill will ask a transient's E, "Can we be finished with this session in sixty minutes?" E usually agrees, and then ends the session exactly at the appointed time. When E does not agree, sessions may last nearly two hours, but Werthauer's principle is seen to work.

The converse of Werthauer's principle is very important. When the transient announces that the session is ended, the observer should ask, "How do you feel?" For if the transient does not feel as well as when the session started, the session is not ended, and the observer must see that the full time needed by E is given.

How is an observer to ask that a session be ended? These words are suitable —

If it is convenient for E to end this session within the next few minutes, we ask that this be done; if it is not convenient, the session may last as long as E wishes.

How often should a transient have sessions? This depends on the type of therapy. It has been found that sessions more often than once in five days may prevent the appearance of fire, as the body needs time to accumulate sufficient energy for fire manifestation. In general, sessions once a week or three times in two weeks seem to bring about integration at a rate which will not be increased by increasing the frequency of sessions.

These statements are valid in a general sense, but the transient's E is the best guide in such matters, or, for that matter, the observer's E.

Some readers have commented that the section on
POSTURING is incomplete; mention should have been
made of yawning, belching, bicycle-riding motions of
the legs, rhythmic poundings of the hands, pelvic
writhings, head-twistings, and much more. The writer certainly was asleep at the switch when this section was written.

Other readers have objected to the benefits offered
in the INVITATION as being too extravagant, especially
the comments about 'genius'. The writer wishes to stress
that the superconscious mind is the source of all prodigies,
just as the conscious mind is the source of all rational
undertakings, and the subconscious mind is the origin
of all that is irrational. We know a number of persons
who have E-sessions for the express purpose of increasing
their creative originality in various arts and sciences,
and we know of a number of creative accomplishments
which are due to E-Therapy.

Some have asked, "What is the legal position of E-
observing?" Please read pages 4 and 68. Here it will
be seen that E is the power referred to as the 'Messiah',
'Saviour', 'the Father Within', 'the Holy Spirit', the 'Comforter',
etc, and it is E who does the therapy, not the observer.
Asking E is equivalent to praying (if properly understood), so an E-observer is a person who utters a

93

prayer on behalf of the transient and then sits with the transient to see how the prayer is answered. We do not know of any state or country in which such a practice is illegal, whether paid for or not. An interesting story of remarkable E-Therapy is 'There Is A River' by Thomas Sugrue, which tells of Edgar Cayce and his extraordinary E-manifestations.

Some have asked, "How can we help the insane?" Use the method described on page 78 — the proxy method. No court or medical authority will ever object to the treatment of confined persons in this way, for no court or medical authority is likely to consider even the possibility of proxy therapy. It isn't even necessary for the observer or proxy-transient to visit the confined person, although it may help in some cases.

Many have wondered about the applications of the superconscious mind to questions other than those of personal integration. We are not in a position to say much about this yet, except that if the ten powers of E can be made available to the human race in all the ways that are already observed in individuals, all of the troubles of the present day will be left far behind. To a small child, an adult seems virtually omniscient. To an average adult, an E-integrated transient will seem so.

An Institute of Integration has been formed to be of service to all persons interested in personal integration and its applications. If you wish to keep up with developments in this field, send a dollar or more to the Institute and you will receive a journal called 'the Integrator'. In the pages of this journal you will learn about lectures, recorded on tape or wire, which are available from the Institute.

For those who respond to it, nothing yet discovered seems better than E-Therapy as described in these pages. But for those who do not respond, promising new E-plus methods have been developed. An excellent method for beginners is 'group-E', for which we are indebted to Junius Adams of San Francisco. 'Teamed hyper-E' was discovered and developed by the friends and family of Edward Robles in Fair Oaks, California, and the writer has trained large groups in the use of this powerful therapy.

'Proxy therapy' (see page 78) was discovered by many persons independently, and it has been demonstrated, by means of electrical instruments, that the tensions of one person <u>can</u> be transferred to another person and there released. 'Insane' persons have been treated with proxy-therapy, and, strange as it may seem, this remarkable power is actually being considered as a remote-control way of removing the emotional and psychological tensions which cause war!

The writer has developed 'E-minus' into a definite therapy which seems helpful to many, and has come forward with a new method called 'E-Suggestion' or ES-Therapy, which consists in using the power of suggestion for the one purpose of improving the transients response to E. This therapy shows promise of producing talents like those of the late Edgar Cayce.

The Institute is making a systematic study of 'psycho-chemistry', which is concerned with the fact that certain vitamins, endocrine extracts, alkaloids and other chemicals are very helpful in slow cases. With all these new methods, there will be no more 'slow' cases, so that access to 'E' will be available for all.

A primary center of integrative study and work is being planned by the Institute, as well as sub-sidiary centers in various city areas throughout the world. With E's help, what <u>can</u> be done <u>will</u> be done.

This book is copyrighted in the United States and internationally by the Institute of Integration (1953).

96

CONTENTS

INVITATION · · · · · · · · ·1
APPROACH · · · · · · · · · ·2
ASKING · · · · · · · · · · ·8
TURN-OFF · · · · · · · · ·23
FIRE · · · · · · · · · · · ·28
TREMOLO · · · · · · · · · ·36
POSTURING · · · · · · · · ·38
HISTORY · · · · · · · · · ·39
STRATEGY · · · · · · · · ·49
ARGUMENT · · · · · · · · ·55
E-PLUS · · · · · · · · · ·73
E-MINUS · · · · · · · · · ·79
QUALIFICATIONS · · · ·87

MWI Publishing
do you have

stories to tell

poems to share

information to impart

then together we will make it happen

www.mwipublishing.com

Visit

http://www.kitselman.com

for details on other material by A. L. Kitselman as well as
further biographical information

If you enjoyed this book you might also like

Mindessence - The Polarity of Life and Death
by Tony Caves
Conditioned by society to live and die in a dream world of our own
making, author Tony Caves offers a pathway to a state of dynamic ease
and alertness. Using simple techniques, drawn from his lifelong interests
in practical philosophy, meditation, Buddhism and martial arts, the book
is a rich tapestry of esoteric teachings.